MARSHALL COUNTY

INDIANA

Amy Lant Wenger

Marshall County Indiana

A Brief History

The History Press

Published by The History Press
Charleston, SC 29403
www.historypress.net

Front cover, top image from the collection of Antiquarian & Historical Society of Culver.

First published 2010

Manufactured in the United States

ISBN 978.1.59629.883.5

Library of Congress CIP data applied for.

Notice: The information in this book is true and complete to the best of our knowledge. It is offered without guarantee on the part of the author or The History Press. The author and The History Press disclaim all liability in connection with the use of this book.

CONTENTS

ACKNOWLEDGEMENTS

There are few sights quite so spectacular as autumn in northern Indiana.

This is the season that was lavished before me as I began my research toward the compilation of this book. Inspiration beckons and surrounds me at every turn: canopies of gold, crimson and amber leaves hover against a backdrop of brilliant blue sky. Gently rolling farmland, now lush with the rewards of the harvest, is rising to meet glorious, blazing dawns and dusks of auburn and rose. It is where I remain awestruck by the magnificence of God's handiwork, the simplicity of the bountiful countryside and the sense of peace that dwells in my heart as I remain now and forever enchanted by the place I still consider my home.

All of this compels me to reflect and reminisce over the journey that brought me to this place and this time in my life, as well as to the amazing people who have illuminated the path I walk along. It is with my heart and soul that I wish to offer my heartfelt sentiments of gratitude to the following individuals and organizations, for it is because of your faith in me and your loyalty and willingness to guide me that this book was made possible. I dedicate and devote each and every word to you all, with love and honor.

For Mrs. Karin Rettinger and the gracious, welcoming staff members of the Marshall County Historical Museum. Where and how can I possibly begin to express my thoughts of how truly indebted I am to your insights and your assistance? My words seem insufficient and inadequate, but I am truly thankful from the depths of my heart. Your enthusiastic and tireless efforts made an intriguing project enlightening and exhilarating at the same time. Bless all of you for everything that you do to preserve the legacy of Marshall County.

For Mr. Jeff Blair, local director for the Lincoln Highway Association. You were one of the first to lend your affirmation to this endeavor from the very beginning, and I am grateful. Many thanks.

For Mr. and Mrs. Larry Lemler. On a sunshine-dappled Sunday afternoon, you astounded me with the intricacy of your lovingly tended museum, and you charmed me with your very apparent devotion to your hometown of Bourbon. What an experience. I will never forget it—or you. Your collections are truly a tremendous asset to your community.

For Ms. Kimberly Berger, clerk-treasurer for the town of Bourbon. Thank you for your thoughtful note of support regarding my work and for helping to put me in touch with the Lemler family.

For Mr. and Mrs. R.T. Henke and Historic Bremen, Inc. Thank you so very much for inviting me into your breathtakingly beautiful home and spending a wonderful day sharing your appreciation of Bremen history with a fellow "Bremenite." I was enthralled by your presence and beyond thrilled to have your support and participation.

For Ms. Marizetta Kenney. I am so appreciative for your friendly and sincere introduction to the Antiquarian and Historical Society of Culver and the Center for Culver History and Research. You were such a delight to correspond with, and I thank you for the time you volunteered on my behalf in search of historic Culver information.

For Mr. Russell J. Lombard, president and CEO of the U.S. Route 6 Tourist Association. Many thanks for providing me with many valuable resources and Internet links, allowing me to rediscover the majestic Grand Army Highway of the Republic (which I was so fortunate to have located virtually in my front yard while growing up in Bremen).

For Mrs. Alice Ridge, author of *Introducing the Yellowstone Trail*. Thank you for sharing your knowledge about a very significant roadway that is seemingly too often underappreciated for its rightful place in history.

For Mr. Kurt Garner, local liaison for the institutions of the Michigan Road and the Lincoln Highway and also a renowned supporter for regional causes supporting historic preservation. I thank you kindly for a very pleasant visit to Java Trail in Plymouth, which yielded a fascinating conversation about your connections to the area, and for offering valuable anecdotes and resources on the illustrious roads of Marshall County.

For Mr. Joseph Gartrell, commissioning editor for The History Press. Thank you for taking a chance on a fellow writer and for believing in my abilities wholeheartedly. Your constant stream of encouragement was a genuine godsend for me. I wish you many more seasons of success.

For the citizens of Marshall County, with particular fondness for the residents of Bremen, both past and present. I was a member of the community for more than twenty years. This was a genuine labor of love for me, and I hope that I have represented Bremen well in this body of work. May you consider this my tribute to you.

For the legacy of my late grandfather, Lloyd William Crawford. I was so young when you left this world for glory in another, but I will always remember how much I was loved by you—the memory of your smile is lovingly etched on my soul. I hope you would be proud of me today.

For my parents, Mr. Robert Lant and Mrs. Karen Crawford Lant. Never once did you ever dissuade me from being anything other than true to my heart, and you provided me with the wings I needed to soar wherever my inclinations would carry me. It is because of your love and passion for history, and your willingness to share it with me, that I truly believe my own interest was stoked. Thank you for loving me and being the most unwaveringly supportive parents a woman could dare to hope or ask for. Know that you are greatly loved, even when my words fail me amidst the power of my own emotions.

For my sister, Sarah Lant Gilmer. We are bound to each other by the love of sisterhood and family, and you are every bit as cherished to me as a dearest friend. I am so honored to have you as such an integral part

Hannah Gabrielle, ten; Rebekah Grace, seven; and Josiah William, three.

of my life; you have left a profound effect on my heart, perhaps in more ways than I could possibly ever express.

For my husband, Larry Dean Wenger Jr. You have always believed in me, and you have been my greatest champion since the time we met more than eighteen years ago. I remain steadfastly convinced, as I was so long ago, that God has sent you to me for a higher purpose and a wondrous calling. May we share many more years of love and faith together, through whatever life challenges us and graces us with along the way.

For my three children, my dearest blessings and angels of my heart. The purity of your sweet souls and kind spirits I will carry with me forever. My life has become alight with such joy and hope since the moments you were born. My daughters, Hannah Gabrielle and Rebekah Grace, and my son, Josiah William—you always have and always will inspire me richly all the days of my life.

And finally for our Heavenly Father, who in his infinite power and wisdom chose to channel in me an enduring passion for expressing all dreams great and small, all thoughts and ideas vast and fleeting, into that which is edifying in his glory. Dear Father, I hope that I have been a faithful and true steward and servant with all that you have bestowed on me.

INTRODUCTION

So the story goes, and so it has been shared in countless ways over decades giving way to centuries, that the man for whom Marshall County is christened never actually walked the hallowed grounds of this fair and fine state. However, in his time, his honorable reputation was regarded as both profound and somewhat providential.

John Marshall was one of America's earliest chief justices among the newly formed Supreme Court, remaining in that position for thirty-four years, an accomplishment that remains one of the longest and most distinguished tenures in political history. An ardent leader and advocate for the Federalist Party, Marshall served as a chief justice from 1801 until his passing in 1835, at the age of seventy-nine. He was lauded for helping to formulate the Constitutional laws of a newly formed nation, was instrumental in establishing a sense of balance within America's early legal system and was highly esteemed for his progressive thinking. His devotion to the causes of his country actually outlived the span of the Federalist Party, whose banner he waved with such conviction.

The region of Marshall County was dictated as such by a statute dated February 7, 1835, just four months before Marshall's death. It was further organized by an act upheld on February 4, 1836, and officially recognized on April 1, 1836. According to the *Register of Officers, Book A* in the Marshall County Courthouse, an election was conducted just three days following to institute a board of commissioners. The three men selected included Robert Blair, who held office from May 1836 until May 1837; Abraham Johnson, who was seated from May 1836 to September 1840; and Charles Osterhout, who had the shortest term at only two months, serving from May 1836 until July of that same year.

Among the earliest orders of business attended to in those formative months was the division of the land into various townships. Only three townships were created initially, but they all bore the familiar names that have carried over into the present day, although greatly extended in terms of size. There were North Township, which today is platted as Polk, German and North Townships; Center Township, now known as West, Center and Bourbon Townships; and Green Township, which currently encompasses Union, Green, Walnut and Tippecanoe Townships.

There is a most interesting anecdote that bears mention as to the somewhat scandalous execution of developing three townships into the ten that are established today. A glance of the current layout of Marshall County details that each of the townships are, for the most part, of uniform design, with a somewhat rectangular configuration. But there is a curious blip along the southeast corner of Polk Township, where a 160-acre section of land should seemingly fall in line with the boundaries of Polk Township but is instead included in the adjacent North Township directly to the east. According to popular folklore, a property owner by the name of Designey Conger was adamantly against the loss of his land to the ensuing acquisition by Polk Township; in accordance with his loyalty to the Whig Party, he felt it was highly inappropriate to allow his land to be transferred unto ownership of a region that bore the name of James K. Polk. Conger held fast to his beliefs and his opposition, and his acreage was left within the North Township configuration. Although there are records to indicate that the land was later transferred to Polk Township, the legendary tale is fascinating all the same.

Of equal fascination and remembrance in the annals and archives of Marshall County is the realization of exactly what and who wandered the land prior to settlement from largely European influences and

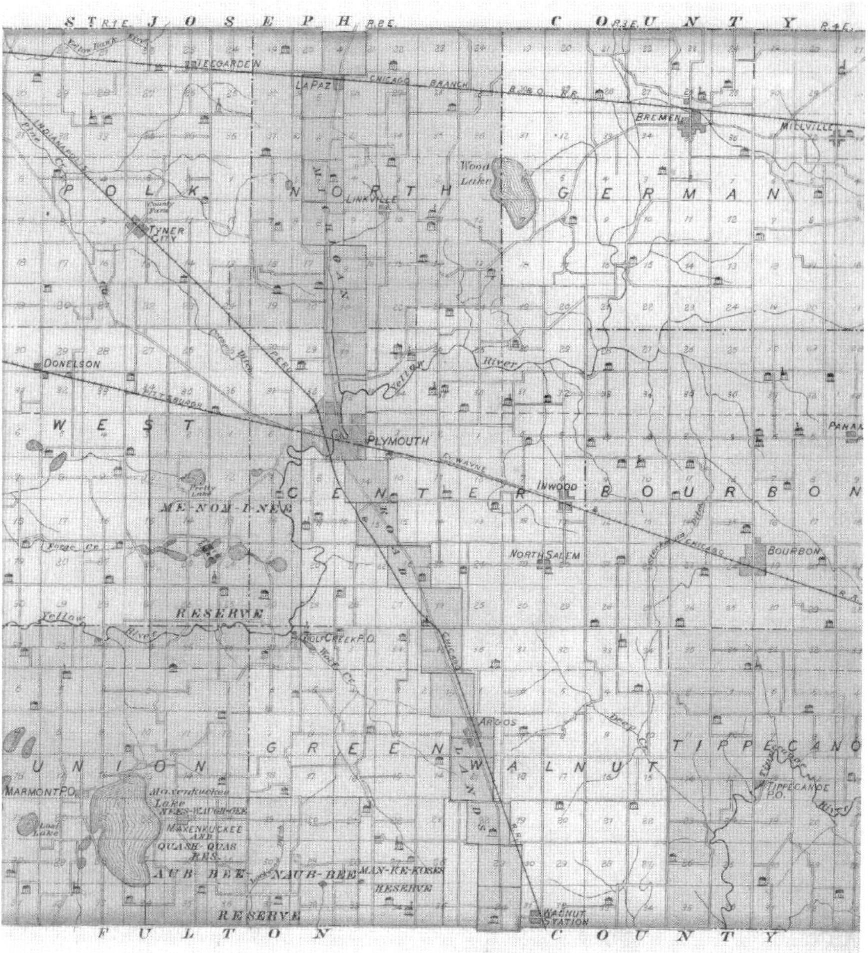

The cities and villages of Marshall County elegantly illustrated on a map—also featuring the ten townships within—as the land appeared in the latter part of the nineteenth century. *Map provided by the Marshall County Historical Museum.*

antecedents. One of the earliest documented cases of the discovery of dinosaur remnants dates back to 1874. The farmstead of Alexander Bland was situated in an area known as Deep Creek in the northeast corner of Walnut Township, near the community of Bourbon. In June 1874, Bland's son, Oscar, was bathing in a pooled tributary of the creek when he stumbled across a large tooth, which was estimated to weigh about eight pounds. Naturally, a great deal of excitement resulted from this discovery, and upon further examination of the creek and its surrounding banks, more bones were revealed.

An officer from the Academy of Sciences of Chicago was summoned to offer expertise on the findings, and upon careful consideration, it was determined that the bones likely belonged to a rather impressively sized mastodon. It was a tale that most certainly traveled about the local circuit for many years beyond and was said to be somewhat embellished over each subsequent retelling, as most folk legends sometimes are.

There have been some residual recordings, historical accounts and books implying that perhaps another group of inhabitants roamed northern Indiana in an era far preceding the county's formation. Later to be called "Mound Builders," it was said that primitive peoples created large hills of dirt that often rose to heights approaching six feet above the surface of the plain. Exactly for what purpose the mounds were meant remains something of a mystery, but it has been largely assumed that the mounds were utilized for burial purposes. In certain instances, however, evidence has also pointed to the possibility that mounds were made for storage of crudely crafted tools. In the latter part of the nineteenth century, some suspiciously rolling land north of Lake Maxinkuckee, near what was then called the "Burr Oak Flats," prompted curiosity among the residents. An expedition of the site revealed such artifacts as arrowheads, pottery and hand tools fashioned from stone, iron and copper. Fragments of human bone were also detected among the mounds. No further records seem to contradict nor confirm the presence of the Mound Builders, but it is generally believed that their presence was known, for however short in duration.

Of course, it must be noted that not only in Marshall County but also in virtually every avenue and facet of the state of Indiana there are the mighty echoes and imprints of the American Indian tribes that once resided here. Although an estimate of exactly when they arrived here is not precisely known, it is generally observed that by the middle part of the eighteenth century, the northern Indiana landscape was inhabited exclusively by American Indians, primarily those of the Miami Confederacy and members of the Potawatomi nation.

As more and more white pioneers arrived in northern Indiana, circumstances would necessitate that there would have to be understandings achieved, and negotiations rendered, as to how these two vastly different populations could possibly share lands in a harmonious manner within the same territory. Eventually, the Potawatomis, whose Indian name translates loosely to "nation of fire blowers," reached a somewhat tentative truce with their white neighbors. By 1828, in an early endeavor to preserve allegiance, the Indians offered the government permission to access a large parcel of land to allow for the construction of the "Michigan Road." Construction for the roadway was underway by 1832, and the roadway remains one of the nation's most heavily traveled and easily recognized early highways, now known as U.S. 31.

Two pivotal treaties would be enacted by the middle part of the 1830s, however, that would seek to have the Potawatomis removed from the northern sector of Indiana. The first stipulation was that the Indians had to move their reservations west of the Mississippi River, thereby relinquishing land rights in their current location. Terms of another, more substantial, provision (enacted in 1836) offered the Indians one dollar per acre, plus an additional trust of 320 acres in Kansas, in exchange for leaving Indiana altogether. This treaty was called the "Treaty of Yellow River." All of the tribal elders signed this clause, with the exception of Chief Menominee, whose tribe remained in the Twin Lakes area. The remaining Potawatomis had two years in which to finally remove the remainder of their tribe members.

Ironically, although Chief Menominee was the lone holdout for conforming to the statutes, his was the tribe remnant thought to have had the best relationship with the new residents. A chapel was constructed near the lone settlement at which, it has been documented, Roman Catholics and American Indians freely worshiped in harmony. A monument heralding the peaceable coexistence that Chief Menominee strived to foster was later fashioned in his memory in 1909.

As an interesting aside, the last known full-blooded American Indian to reside in Marshall County was Otwan Onago, better known to the neighbors of his homeland as Anthony Nigo. Because he was of half-Miami and half-Potawatomi descent, he was exempt from the mandate to leave the region, as the order was only dictated to full-blooded Potawatomi members. He was born sometime in 1805 and died on

March 19, 1877. He was baptized into the Catholic faith in 1828 and was a missionary who had a homestead in Bourbon Township, owning eighty acres along the northwest corner of Fir Road and 9B Road. He later established residency in Plymouth before his passing and was laid to rest at St. Michael's Cemetery in Plymouth.

It was said to be a very bittersweet time in northern Indiana when General John Tipton and his comrades arrived in 1838 to ensure that the final Indians would be forcibly removed from Marshall County. On the Sunday prior to their departure, the white settlers and their families came to realize that their Indian predecessors were trusted allies and were visibly saddened by the impending turn of events as they bade their friends farewell. About 770 Potawatomi families from the Marshall County area, many of whom were sickly and later perished along the westward exodus, were finally shepherded away during a weeklong

The solemn, simple orchestration from the "Slumber Song of a Vanished Race," composed during and inspired by the events of the "Trail of Death," during which the last of the Potawatomi Indians were removed from northern Indiana in 1838. *Excerpt derived from* A Twentieth Century History of Marshall County, Indiana, *published by the Honorable Daniel McDonald, 1908.*

period between August 30 and September 3, 1838, an event later termed the "Trail of Death."

The somber pilgrimage to Kansas was memorialized in the lyrical lamentation shown here, the chants and melody composed by an unknown author. In an article published shortly before his death in 1899, Simon Pokagon, chief to a small band of Potawatomis near Holland, Michigan, pondered the future of his people: "So there must come a time when, leaving no trace behind, he shall pass out of this world, when the 'last Indian' shall go…like the mist."

More than 170 years after the last of the Potawatomi Indians left for Kansas, traces of their influence still resonate strongly in northern Indiana. Many area landmarks, formations of natural phenomena and other touchstones of importance still bear the original names christened by the Indians who first triumphed in their discovery, although they are more commonly known and referred to by their English translations today.

With such a remarkable historic legacy duly chronicled, it certainly seems quite fitting that Marshall County is typically thought of, indeed, as the crossroads of America. It not only considered as such from a perspective of its proximity to the great midwestern heartlands, but it is also truly a place where the past, present and future are respected and celebrated with the highest regard of honor.

CHAPTER 1
ARGOS

A Rustic Turnstile on a Path Most Traveled

Perhaps it was a trace of serendipity, and a hint of future prosperity, that beckoned the first settlers to the lands that would eventually become the town of Argos.

It was in the earliest part of the 1830s that the region was undergoing a period of significant transformation. The workings of a treaty had recently been ratified between the Potawatomi Indians and the white pioneers, which would dictate the terms of removing the American Indians from northern Indiana and relocating them to new homelands westward. Another resolution had been newly executed in which the Potawatomis offered a large parcel of land to begin construction of a thoroughfare to be called the Michigan Road. This land was later sold to the new settlers about 1832, and the ensuing project was deemed to be a tremendous undertaking that would revolutionize travel. The means by which the Michigan Road came to fruition will be touched on in a later chapter of the book.

So it was likely that there was a great deal of anticipation and foresight within the minds of the first families to establish farms and homesteads along the rapidly evolving landscape. The first man to discover the potential of settlement along this site was Abel Hickman, who arrived in October 1832 and set about constructing a cabin about two and a half miles south of present-day Argos. He was followed shortly thereafter by Michael Shone, whose home was erected six miles south of the current town boundaries, and Judge Polk (also listed as "Polke"), who built a home along the northeast branch of the Tippecanoe River in Fulton County.

The following year, in 1833, Sidney Williams made his presence known by launching himself headlong into an entrepreneurial mindset. He purchased six hundred acres of land and set about clearing a wide swath for the formation of the Michigan Road. Williams's property was adjacent to that of another newcomer by the name of Caleb Railsback. Williams was also the creator and proprietor of the settlement's first tavern and hotel, which became a most popular place for social gatherings. Williams moved from the region sometime about 1848, but not before leaving an admirable reputation, according to the early Argos archives. He was the first associate judge of the circuit court from 1836 to 1843 but was drawn to the state of California by the promise of the gold rush and the riches said to be in abundance there.

Prior to his departure, Williams sold his ownerships to Clark Bliven, the man credited with building the courthouse. The inn was later sold to Dr. Cailat, a French native who built the Kelly House in the 1860s.

A sweeping glance along the South Maple Avenue corridor near downtown Argos, in this undated image circa the early 1900s. Looking north, one can distinguish the home of the Barr family in the foreground at right, one of Argos's oldest houses. The Congregational Church building is seen in the left corner, and just beyond it, the home of C.E. Alleman. *Marshall County Historical Museum.*

According to early recollections, the first Argos cemetery was created along South Michigan Street where Memorial Park now stands. When a traveler at the Williams' Inn died during his stay in 1838, it was easily recognized that there would be a need to procure a suitable spot for burial. In short order, a gathering of walnut trees was cut down, resulting in the makeshift cemetery, and the deceased was laid to rest in the northeast corner, where the south end of Maple Street now winds.

As the years ambled on, more folks arrived to discover the prospect of settlement in a land where plentiful woods, waters and wildlife sufficed well for a pioneer way of life. The organization of churches and schools came about as the population inched upward. The first documented schoolhouse was believed to have been built circa 1847 and was situated on the southwest corner of the current Memorial Park. The "little red schoolhouse," aptly named on account of the weathered rustic façade, comprised one singular room. Among those entered in the list of early educators were Peter D. Lowe, Malinda Brown and Wesley Blodgett. A second schoolhouse, a white frame structure, was to follow by the early 1870s, located on Cemetery Street.

The first school to carry a group of students along the path to eventual commencement was built in 1873 and was located on Cemetery Street between Maple and Michigan Streets. The new facility was priced at $8,000 and featured six rooms with plainly outfitted windows, double-seated desks, a central stairway, stove heating and a majestic belfry, among other amenities. The first graduating class of students consisted of five pupils in 1883. Twenty-seven other students completed their course of studies in the new schoolhouse, until March 16, 1892, when the building was consumed by fire. In rapid succession, a new building was constructed directly on the same site, with major additions of an auditorium, stage and gymnasium being included in 1926.

The residence of Abel Hickman was said to be one of the first local havens calling neighbors together in fellowship, as he welcomed followers of faith into his home for many years. By 1844, Hickman donated a parcel of farmland for the purpose of building a permanent house of worship, one of the first in the fledgling burg. The second incarnation of the community schoolhouse also served a dual purpose as an early church, until such time as a larger schoolhouse became necessary, and then the stately little schoolhouse became a serviceable place of gathering for worshipers of many denominations.

On January 8, 1851, the duo of John Pleak and Marquis L. Smith finally set about drafting boundaries about the land to officially establish a town, which they called Sidney, owing to the remembrance of one of the first trailblazing residents of the area. The site, which boasted sixty lots, was surveyed and platted by Amasa W. Reed. Sidney was the hub for the region's postal services for three years following, until political motivations led to its removal by 1854. In 1856, twenty-six lots were cobbled together for the provenance of an additional town. The final plat was laid out on November 6, 1856, by Joseph H. Rhodes, who chose the name of Fremont to celebrate Colonel John C. Fremont's appointment as a presidential candidate on the Republican ticket. Needless to say, though, upon Fremont's defeat in his presidential bid, it became rather apparent that perhaps the honor of naming a town for him may have been presumptuous.

By this time, impending issues of concern included how to address the conundrum of having two settlements almost directly adjacent to each other. Rumblings were beginning to reverberate among the local residents that it was "against the interest of the citizens of said places" to continue to function as two independent communities. Therefore, a decision was rendered by the powers of what was then called Green Township to recognize and rename the two hamlets as one. A meeting was announced for May 21, 1859, that would take place at the local schoolhouse and be open to the general public. The small audience was led by de facto president Merrill Williams and de facto secretary Samuel B. Corbelay. The matters of the agenda included appointing a trustee within the formation of a new township and christening the resulting city of unification.

Names that were bandied about for consideration of the community were Richland, Noble and Argos. The latter was a suggestion from Schuyler Colfax, who was a congressman of the district. Colfax, famously fascinated with elements of Greek history, derived the name from the ancient city cited in Homer's *Iliad*. By a final tally of thirteen votes for Argos and eight for Richland, and with the name of Noble withdrawn, the order to consolidate was carried forth, and the city thereafter was called Argos.

Walnut Township was the chosen name to replace that of Green, presumably due to the large proliferation of walnut trees that were scattered about the region, as no other known reason was proffered as to why the name of Walnut was selected. The date listed for the institution of Walnut Township is June 9, 1859.

John A. Rhodes secured the most votes in a subsequent contest as township trustee, soundly beating his opponent, Charles Brown, by a tally of eighteen to four. A trio of individuals, including Merrill Williams, John A. Rhodes and N.E. Manville, was advised to bring the new order for the organization for presentation before the existing board of commissioners.

The city of Argos was incorporated unto state law in December 1869, and on the fourth day of the month, an election was held to seat a slate of officers. Those who were led to oversee the city were Joseph F. Norton, Jonathan Pickerel and J.S. Leland, trustees; James Pickerel, town marshal; George W. Krouse, clerk; A. Seely, treasurer; and W.R. Cook, assessor.

As the later decades of the nineteenth century passed, Argos was keeping pace quite well with the task of recruiting new businesses and

A scene along the Walnut Street thoroughfare, looking westward, in a moment captured from the first years of the twentieth century. *Marshall County Historical Museum.*

other social causes to the city. Greatly energized, surely, by the rapidly advancing conduit of the Michigan Road highway, such enterprises as the General Store of Hagan Brothers, Martin Bucher & Son and other notable early endeavors were soon well ensconced into their niches. Other businessmen whose names were later etched into prominence for their civic contributions were Railsback, Lowry, Worthington and Huff, many of whose descendants still remain deeply affirmed to their hometown.

Milestones continued to appear along the timeline of Argos's evolution. About 1865, the Indianapolis, Peru and Chicago Railroad, which connected LaPorte to the city of Plymouth, was slated for extension. Folks were greatly anticipating the possibility of having a branch of a major railroad passing just steps from their business district and expeditiously sought to have their town included in the lineup of potential stops. Three years passed before the people of Argos received the service for the "Peewee line," as it was commonly called, which allowed the city to restore postal service up to three deliveries per week. Legendary tales talk of the festive mood about town when the first steam engine arrived gracefully along a gleaming set of tracks in 1868.

A smattering of new businesses soon took advantage of the junction placement, most notably Merl Williams & Son's Elevator. When another advancement in the rail line came about in 1882 with the creation of the Nickel Plate Railroad, Argos was among the few towns that were able to offer daily mail service.

The 1870s saw the formation of a civic band, which rightfully took its place alongside a wealth of factories, lumber and flouring mills, a wagon factory and other ventures that composed the workings of the town. Another pivotal event occurred in Argos on May 13, 1878, with the formation of the Marshall County Medical Society. Charter members installed that day were Drs. Samuel W. Gould, Reason B. Eaton, J.H. Wilson, J.S. Leland, F. Stevens and J.T. Doke. The mission of the society was outlined to "be for the purpose of advancing medical knowledge, and to elevate professional character."

With the building boom of Argos still very much underway by the 1880s, there came a catastrophic occurrence that threatened to devastate the very heart of the city. In January 1887, a massive inferno erupted along eleven of the storefronts that lined the west side of the South Michigan Street corridor. The winter weather, rather than creating a hindrance in warding off the blaze, proved to be of some benefit, as most of the connected buildings were blanketed with more than a foot of snow at the time, which helped to stave off widespread damage. The conditions were such that the proprietors were swiftly able to remove many of their wares and merchandise with minimal loss. It was said that because Argos was becoming so widely realized as a place to launch new businesses, the resulting empty lots were worth more after the flames were extinguished than they had been prior to the fire.

Even so, the town trustees wasted little time in drafting an ordinance prohibiting the further construction of wooden structures within the city limits. The hollowed-out shells of timber fragments and frames were soon replaced by brick buildings and façades, the greater share of which still reign regally along the streets of downtown Argos.

Another section of beautifully designed homes in olden times of central Argos, with the former residence of William Schoonover seen in the foreground. *Marshall County Historical Museum.*

As Argos crossed over the threshold into the twentieth century, so with it followed the specters of war and conflict, through which the town saw a fair share of sacrifice, honor and bravery from those who gave selflessly of themselves for the means of a greater good. Argos lost three comrades during the First World War—Donald Clark Bryan, James Lowell Corey and Glen D. Sherland. Losses were greater over the Second World War, with the passing of Ora R. Bolinger, Norbert Burkett, Robert C. Davis, Donald D. Fishburn, Robert Fishers, Dwight Grossman, Lamoine E. Jordan, Anthony Macukas, Robert B. Miller, John C. Mitchell, Kenneth Pontius, Ambrose Sissel, Billie L. Staner, Richard E. Street, Basil Thompson, Edgar Treber and Robert Warren. And lastly, one final soldier perished during the Korean War—John Miller.

So many years later, now with the advent of the twenty-first century, Argos still maintains its original spirit as a place of new beginnings while holding dearly to the traditions that have shaped its existence. Melvin Lake Corey, an Argos native, was elected as the first secretary of the National Retail Hardware Association in 1901, setting his national "headquarters" in the confines of the Corner Hardware building. However small the office space is, it served as a powerful hub for the organization's connections across the country, and the new notoriety sparked yet another influx of business to the town.

The Izaak Walton League issued its affiliation to an Argos membership of sixty-eight individuals in 1926, with the building designated for club purposes created in 1932. The group earned distinction in 1936 by becoming the smallest charter for raising the most game fish, 22,294, raised within a private hatchery—the first time such a feat had been accomplished by any league denomination east of the Mississippi River.

The middle portion of the twentieth century saw the unveiling of a new public library, a weeklong fair sponsored by the Argos Lions Club and the Argos centennial celebration of 1951. By 1955, the Argos Community School System was created by merging the rural schools from Green and Walnut Townships, with both districts moving to new facilities by 1957. A new grocery store, auto showroom, medical clinic, sewer system and post office were included in the commerce highlights of the 1960s, and the former town cemetery, which had been left to deteriorate along the

The famed and fabled Izaak Walton Clubhouse in Argos, center of much fanfare during its inception and beyond, as it appeared circa 1957. *From the historical photograph archives of Amy Wenger.*

The downtown business sector, changing pace with the times, in this circa 1940s image. The Argos State Exchange Bank holds a prestigious position at the intersection. *Marshall County Historical Museum.*

Michigan Road, was razed to make way for a greenway. A children's playground, sponsored by the Junior Civic League, was later built nearby. Federal grant monies were gifted to Argos in the 1970s, allowing for the creation of Argonaut Park, an industrial neighborhood, which was formally dedicated on July 2, 1976. More federal grant monies fueled another pivotal town project in 1978: the institution of an emergency volunteer medical service, which furnished Argos with an ambulance and related lifesaving equipment.

An award-winning high school athletics program has garnered recognition in fairly recent years, including three IHSAA soccer championships in 1973, 1976 and 1978. Meanwhile, the boys' basketball squad, during the years spanning 1972 to 1981, amassed an incredible overall record of 171 wins and only 43 losses, an achievement led by legendary coach Phil Weybright.

Today, Argos is a bustling small town of about 1,700 residents, a charming enclave within southern Marshall County. It is now left to future generations to continue on with the history yet to be revealed about the winsome town of Argos, Indiana.

CHAPTER 2

BOURBON

Innovation and Industry, Blazing a Righteous Trail

When Indiana was formalized as the nineteenth state of the Union in 1816, a great many of the newly minted Hoosiers sought to linger farther downstate to start businesses and raise homesteads, farms and families, as well as pursue related interests. Slowly but surely, the intrigue of largely untapped resources, new settlements and transportation advancements piqued the interest of pioneers. It is thought that this is the spirit that compelled travelers to meander about to parts northbound in search of a new sense of perspective.

Among those who can be counted in the movement were two men who purchased land in Bourbon Township in the closing months of 1835. The first individual on record to have purchased land in the region was Charles C. Hardy, who in September 1835 procured 240 acres in the vicinity of South Beech Road and East Fourteenth Road. Later that year, by December, Hardy would have a neighbor in William Blakely, who purchased 80 acres near the juncture of East 12B Road and South Elm Road. Both landowners were able to negotiate their price at $1.25 per acre.

In the two years that followed, eighty-seven additional property rights were sold to interested parties. However, there were conditions to be met—the new owners were required to clear away the land and handle relevant drainage issues that plagued the woodsy, swampy countryside, which may well have contributed to why the Potawatomi Indians commonly referring to the region as the "Land of the Fireflies." A large number of these frontier-minded settlers were onetime residents of Bourbon County, Kentucky, and so the new township would be named similarly in a nod to their former living place. Among the earliest documented pioneers to become residents in the region were families by the names of Parks, Greer and Linn.

The year of formal organization for Bourbon Township is listed as 1840 and, at the time, included a small portion of what is now Tippecanoe Township. The latter would break away and form its own township just two years later, and the original boundaries for the town of Bourbon were drawn in 1853, with incorporation to occur in 1865.

In those days, not everyone was quite so willing to subject themselves to the grueling task of clearing their newly acquired acreage, which many folks had admittedly negotiated sight unseen. Many of those early pioneer families were driven to forage and fend for themselves by way of sheer willpower, and walking was by far the preferred means of travel. There were a few crudely patterned trails that crisscrossed through the

The United Brethren Church of Bourbon was one of the community's first houses of worship. *Larry Lemler.*

county, as was illustrated in an 1850s map showing the first phase of the Michigan Road nearby, the Plymouth-Goshen Trail, the Plymouth-LaPorte Trail and the Plymouth-Leesburg Road. There were also traces of a path leading from a Chippewa settlement near Rochester extending northeastward to Elkhart, as well as another that originated in the South Bend area and passed through the present-day site of Bourbon. It is evident that remnants from some of the older variations of these trails ran concurrently with trails that ran through a wooded area between 14B and Fifteenth Roads. A vast curvature of land found among the trees was said to serve as a "natural amphitheatre" at which the Potawatomis held their council meetings. It is located at the current farmstead of Will Erwin and remains proportionate to the bowl-shaped dimensions said to be carved from glacier movements long ago. Many of Bourbon's townspeople believe that there is a second such formation at the top of Summit Chapel behind the cemetery.

Before the first stakes were planted for the creation of the eventual town of Bourbon itself, one local resident achieved a bit of notoriety in Hoosier headlines. The first college-educated man from Marshall County originated from Bourbon Township, a fellow by the name

Downtown Bourbon, featuring a long view of the Center Street neighborhood, in a photo taken about 1908. *Larry Lemler.*

of John F. Parks. His experience was made possible through the efforts of his father, James Parks, who petitioned Indiana College of Bloomington to permit his son to further his studies there, following a two-year course of study. Parks's application was accepted on March 7, 1837.

To that end, it was apparent that many of Bourbon Township's preeminent first citizens were very well educated and served their communities as schoolteachers, while schools rose up in quick succession within the grid of farms and homesteads. The first known school was of a primitive sort, taught by Edward Parks and initiated in 1838 with a class consisting of six pupils. An early local history places a log cabin structure "90 rods" west of Center and Main, which places it along the Leesburg Road, or 12B Road, near the old cemetery west of town. It was used between 1848 and 1854.

Another early public school that served the children residing within city limits was built in 1865–66, although its precise location is uncertain. An 1872 map of the town designates a schoolhouse perched on the southwest corner of Clay and Main Streets, so it is assumed that this is the building in question.

One of the first public school buildings to house the students of Bourbon, as it looked in 1911. *Larry Lemler.*

Rural institutions of learning were of extreme value to Bourbon and the surrounding township residents, as there was an unusually high number of country schoolhouses chronicled on record by the closing years of the 1800s. In 1890, there were no fewer than eighteen one-room district schools scattered about the region. Youthful scholars of the era typically embarked on an eight-year passage of study, culminating with a graduation service commemorating the conclusion of grade eight. Participation in such exercises was dependent on the passage of a rigorous examination, which touched on such subject matter as physiology, geography, music appreciation, agriculture and industrial arts, as well as solid comprehension of the "basics."

The town also has a unique footnote in local history with regards to higher education. At a certain point of time during the ending years of the twentieth century, the community hosted the Salem College and the Bourbon College and School of Music. Unfortunately, neither campus reigned for any significant period of time. When the Bourbon College disbanded in 1877, the building was given to the use of the town as a public school.

Salem College was begun as a United Brethren institution but was dissolved before the first student was ever enrolled. The Northern Indiana German Baptists tried to take the reins later on, restoring the Salem College name, but this incarnation only lasted a handful of years before folding due to lack of support. Frank Reubelt then expressed an interest in reopening the college, this time calling it the Bourbon College, but it also fell victim to inexperience and was closed by about 1878. The Salem/Bourbon College was located at the east end of, appropriately, College Street and is currently the site of the elementary school playground. Many of the bricks from the old building were salvaged and used in the construction of the home for Reverend Cecil.

Bourbon's final attempt to organize a secondary school was the Bourbon School of Music, which was located in the southern part of town and existed for a short duration beginning from about 1900 and ending after three or four years.

Because young Bourbon was still thickly populated with an overabundance of walnut and poplar trees, it seemed a logical progression

The structure that once housed the Bourbon College, before being revived as a public school building near the late 1870s. *Larry Lemler.*

to take advantage of the situation by allowing the lumbering industry to fall in line at the forefront of business growth. When a new section of the Pennsylvania rail service crossed through the land by 1856, this quickly facilitated the usage of the line for the shipment of lumber, which was said to be siphoned through the community by thousands of carloads annually. Whatever timber remained in excess about town was generally put to use through other means—for the construction of cabins, storefronts and framings, sawmills and makeshift walkways. And whatever trees could not be put to some valuable use were burned as excess; there simply were not enough mills to clear the land at a fast-enough pace for the growing numbers of farmers.

Some of the area's earliest industries also spun off from tangents pertaining to woodworking, and employment opportunities were plentiful for a great many of the men in residence. The first documented business structure built in the town square was a log building at the northeast juncture of Main and Center Streets, a general store owned and operated by William E. Thompson. Other early ventures that were situated along the Main Street lineup in following years were James Nichols's meat market, a saloon owned by Thomas Banks and

The former Pennsylvania depot as it was about 1910, when Bourbon was still regarded as a pivotal juncture on the line. *Larry Lemler.*

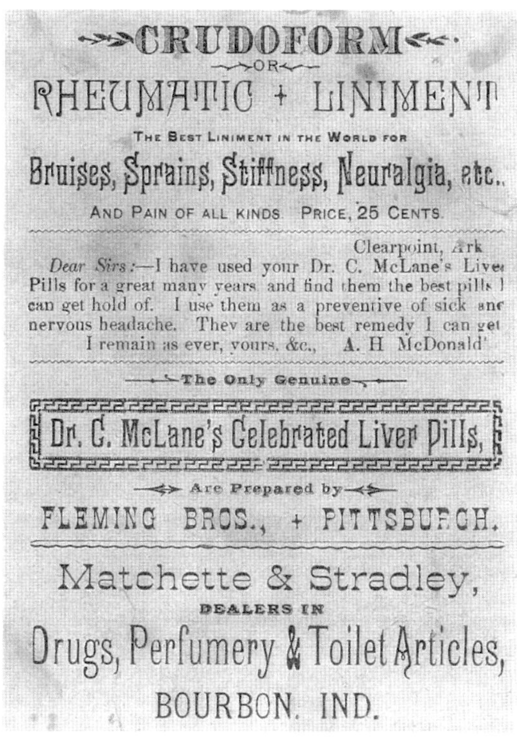

This early advertisement, promoting the use of "liver pills" for the improvement of health and well-being, was sponsored by pharmacy owners Matchette and Stradley of Bourbon. *Clipping courtesy of Mr. Larry Lemler.*

operated by Philip Matz, the offices of Drs. Matchett and France, Leroy Manville's grocery, D. Walmer's shoe shop, J. Oldfather's daguerrian rooms, the office of Dr. Johnson, the H.A. Snep grocery and bakery and A.W. Johnson's barbershop. John Baxter is listed as the town's first blacksmith, opening his operation in 1859, and Glingle's Harness Shop also appreciated brisk business, along with carriage and wagon makers, coopers, tinsmiths and cobblers.

One of Bourbon's largest and most highly patronized businesses of the closing years of the 1890s was Fribley's Department Store, started by brothers James and Fred Fribley and their sister, Lizzie Fribley Brillhart, a milliner. The store carried a tremendous wealth of wares ranging from groceries, apparel, dry goods, meats and produce. During its heyday at the rise of the 1900s, it was generally called the "shopping center" of the county. The store was eventually sold in 1930 and became Cloud's Department Store.

One of the area's most uniquely adorned early businesses, it was not hard to determine what the focus of this venture was—this was "salting station 25" for Heinz pickles, formerly located in Bourbon. There were a number of similar pickling and salting stations scattered about Marshall County, including sites in Argos, Tyner and Donaldson. Farmers of the region grew specific types of cucumber seeds, which were nurtured in growth to proper proportions and then harvested for use at the pickling plants. *Larry Lemler.*

An undated photograph of the old Colonial Hotel of Bourbon. *Larry Lemler.*

Those who had cause to wander through the region were never far from lodging facilities in downtown Bourbon. The first of these was known as the Baxter Hotel, which was located at the southeast corner of the Main Street square and opened in 1854. The hotel prided itself on granting guests a great range of amenities not typically found during that particular time. Some years later, a new brick building rose up at the site, and the hotel established its new locale east, directly across the alley, where it remained until it was replaced by a shoe shop operated by Charles Snyder. A number of additional hotels and boarding rooms—including the Zouave House, the Rice House and the Colonial Hotel—were strategically situated near the heart of the city as well as the railroad.

Sadly, many of those founding businesses suffered extreme losses during an inordinately large number of catastrophic fires that transpired during the middle years of the twentieth century. The Thompson building, the first business erected in Bourbon, burned down in 1854. Much of the aforementioned business sector was lost to a fire that decimated an entire block in 1872. Other landmarks lost to flames included the N.D. Hellar and Nicholas Galentine flour mills and the Odd Fellows building in 1863, a church and the public school building in 1864 and the Davis mills in 1865. Beal's Saloon and a stable owned by Mr. Cless were swept away by flames in 1872. The axe handle factory and the private residence of Peter Kniseley, who then owned one of the first houses built in Bourbon, were both consumed in 1878, and a large expanse of buildings near the Bourbon Opera House was reduced to ashes in 1885. The opera house itself was spared through the grace of shifting winds.

Such a great many fires occurring within a relatively brief span of time most surely kept busy the men of the Vigilant Hook and Ladder Company, the first firefighting organization called to serve the people of Bourbon, beginning in 1875.

In 1864, Bourbon welcomed the creation of a telegraph office, which permitted another means of communication and a window to the world beyond the township boundaries. The local office was considered of great importance on the line that connected Fort Wayne to Chicago, as Bourbon was quickly earning a reputation for its stellar lumbering capacities. Another impetus to remain relevant to the evolving times was

The members of the volunteer brigade of Bourbon's Hook & Ladder Company as they were in 1896. *From left:* Joe Orr, Jacob Wigman, Will Lawrence, Dode Denoss, Omar Stough, Lewis Glingle, Frank Caul, Ed Brilliant, Austin Downing, Harry Alwein, Will Kehler, Willard Lawrence, Lloyd Lynch, George McCoy, Bert Tyrrell, Will Glingle, Ed Garrison, Charles Glingle, Curt Wachter, Newt Mowery, Will Wilt, Till Gunn (at base of ladder), Ted O'Brien and Blair Lawrence (on back of wagon). The photo was taken at the residence of J.H. Matchett and Dr. Marshall Iden, on North Main Street. *Larry Lemler.*

the formulation of print media. Several newspapers were presented as representations for local and regional events, beginning with the short-lived *Bourbon Independent* in 1865. That publication would be succeeded by Ignatious Mattingly's *Bourbon Mirror* of 1871; the *Bourbon Review* of 1879; the *Bourbon Democrat*, printed each Saturday beginning in 1882; the *Bourbon Bitters*, which focused on humor; and the *Gospel Messenger*. The *Bourbon Record* had perhaps the shortest tenure of the lot, lasting just one month during the year 1884—that is, unless one considers a brief news appearing in an 1894 issue of the *Plymouth Republican*, which makes mention of a new Bourbon paper to be called the *Midway Plaisance*. That was the first, and last, known appearance of that publication, taking its unusual name "plaisance" from a term meaning park or garden.

Above all of the fledgling publications that came and went over time, the *Bourbon News-Mirror* was the one that reigned in longevity, bowing in the 1890s as simply the *Bourbon News* and founded by the Harris

This grouping of dapper and distinguished fellows composed an early incarnation of the Bourbon Band, in what was most likely the late 1800s. An inscription on the back of the photograph identifies the men as, *from left*, Ora Shumaker, Phil Steinman, Sam Lemler, Clarence Lemler, Don Shumaker, Vern Snyder, Dobbin Hibbets, Dr. Fuller, Norm Neisley and Sam Bristol. Mark Swoverland is designated the snare drummer, while Frank Dinica is the bass drummer. *Larry Lemler.*

brothers. In time, Mattingly's earlier publication, the *Mirror*, merged with that of the *News*, thus creating the *Bourbon News-Mirror*. The publication remains a valuable resource of community information and is still distributed weekly under the ownership of the Pilot News, a Plymouth-based institution that oversees the organization of several area weekly and daily newspapers.

To indulge in a moment of respectful digression, it would seem an appropriate opportunity to share something more of the life of local resident Anthony Nigo, the last known full-blooded Indian resident of Marshall County, whose presence in Bourbon Township was alluded to earlier. Nigo, whose American Indian name was Otwan Onago, was permitted to remain in residence beyond the time of the Potawatomi Indians' departure in 1838, exempted from the order because of his mother's Miami Indian descent.

Nigo enjoyed a respectable and congenial rapport with his fellow Bourbon residents and was widely regarded as a peaceable man of faith. Records indicate that Nigo was born in Kosciusko County in 1805 and purchased land near Tippecanoe Town from Stephen Benack about 1828, the same year that he was baptized into the Catholic faith. He was married to his bride, known to the locals as Angeline, at about this same time, in a ceremony held at the Twin Lakes Indian chapel.

Though the couple had no children together, Angeline entered into the union with a son, who was known as Peter Shipshewana. The honor of Nigo's faith and family were of the utmost importance to him, as was detailed in a tragic event that occurred in early 1854. An intruder entered the Nigo home near his property at Fir and 9B Roads, about five miles northeast of Bourbon. During the scuffle that followed, young Peter was knocked to the floor, with the vagrant subsequently threatening to kill the lad with the next blow he delivered. Nigo shot and killed the man to save the boy he considered with heart and soul to be his own son.

The matter was discussed by way of a formal inquest that took place in late April by a committee composed of John C. Hedrick, Jonas C. Mooney, Henry H. Baxter, Daniel Studebaker, Marvin Hamilton and Francis Kincade—a grouping of "six good and lawful men in said township." It was the overwhelming consensus of the gentlemen that

This is a vintage scene from the grounds of the William Acker sawmill, with a handful of workers seen near the left, from about the 1890s. *Marshall County Historical Museum.*

Nigo's actions were driven by his desire to protect his family and that no laws were deemed violated as a result.

Nigo's Bourbon homestead consisted of eighty acres along the northwest corner of Fir and 9B Roads. In his later life, Nigo relocated to a residence near St. Michael's Catholic Church in Plymouth to become more active in the church community there. Nigo passed away on March 19, 1877, and was laid to rest in the northeast sector of the St. Michael's Cemetery, where a number of former priests were also buried.

Not lost to the early citizens of Bourbon was the importance of establishing itself as a place to look for fine arts and other cultural outlets. One of the very first experiments into such causes was the formation of the Bourbon Cornet Band in 1866. Also, given the vast array of schoolhouses scattered about the township, many of the buildings were often utilized for church functions, town meetings, musical presentations and club gatherings.

One of the most fêted events in the annals of local lore was the Bourbon Fair, which was a highly anticipated annual spectacle that drew visitors from miles around. The installation of the fair dates back to 1872 with the organization of the Pioneer Farmers Club. Harrison Sparrow was the group president and Washington Iden, the secretary. John Iden, Jeptha Disher and William E. Gay also coordinated additional details. The premiere festival was a modest affair even for the era—no entry fee was charged nor any premiums paid; only simple ribbons were given as reward to a spartan few exhibitors. It was held at the No. 9 Schoolhouse, then located about one and a half miles east of Bourbon, in October 1872.

Eventually, the festival gained sponsorship, support and enthusiasm from a broader spectrum, and the fair came to include a carnival, food and craft vendors, horse racing and, of course, agricultural displays featuring the latest trends in farming equipment.

For several decades beyond, the fair was always conducted during one week of October, with Wednesday designated as a "school day." On

Spectators create an impressively large crowd en masse during the heyday of the Bourbon Fair in 1909. *Larry Lemler.*

that occasion, a parade of floats would be on display, boasting the proud artistic talents of the area schoolchildren. Thursday was often the day that marked the highest number of people in attendance, often crossing the ten thousand mark.

Several changes were implemented in later years in the name of enhancing the fairgrounds, including the installation of floodlights and fencing for the racetrack in 1957. The previous year, plans for the annual school parade were scrapped when the date of the fair was pushed back to August so as not to interfere with the 4-H Fair that was occurring in nearby Argos. Residents were soundly displeased by the loss of the parade, and so it was reinstated as a fair attraction one year later. The fairgrounds were typically rented out for other purposes around the calendar year in an effort to secure additional revenue, so it was not uncommon to find circus performances, exotic horse shows and flower exhibitions taking place at any given time.

Attendance continued to decline into the 1960s, and by 1963, it was decided by the fair's governing association to offer the fairgrounds for a lease arrangement to any interested party that might be willing to take over ownership. In August 1963, by a vote of twenty-seven to nine, the remaining stockholders made a motion to sell the land to the newly formed Tri-Township United School Corporation for the amount of $31,000. The Bourbon Fair Association legally disbanded in February 1964, and the final elements of the regal grandstand were at last razed in 1966.

The proliferation of lush woods and abundant timber was substantially thinning by the first half of the 1900s, and so it seemed like a feasible solution to make way for agriculture as a more reliable means of livelihood for many residents. Municipal services were added to accommodate the needs of the growing number of farm families, including the addition of a telephone exchange, city water, a town bank, paved roads and electricity—promptly turned off by execution of an 11:00 p.m. curfew.

The passage of years ushered in other milestones, such as the consolidation of public and township schools, definitively ending the chapter of the one-room schoolhouse for Bourbon. A new school building was unveiled in 1918 to house all of the local students, and it served for a

Bourbon's Main Street corridor, as viewed from above in 1913. *Larry Lemler.*

Two women grace the front entrance of the Federal Café in a picture captured presumably in the early part of the twentieth century. *Larry Lemler.*

decade until a fire on Christmas Eve 1928 reduced the facility to rubble. Only a short time passed before a newer structure was completed and education resumed.

Happenings transpired at a fast and furious pace in the 1920s, beginning that first year of the decade, when an outbreak of Spanish influenza struck the community of Bourbon with such severity that the local newspapers devoted many weeks and many columns of space to the listing of those who were casualties of the illness. The automobile boom necessitated the opening of the town's first service station in 1924, by the brothers Jesse and Fred Gerard. The business captured headlines again just months later when an intruder blew open the company safe and absconded with an astronomical sum of cash nearing $10,000. In 1953, that same business was targeted again, and again the losses were tallied at about $10,000.

The Bourbon Knights baseball squad, assembled for a team photograph in 1908. *Larry Lemler.*

A number of Bourbon's women rallied together to form the Women's Christian Temperance Union in 1925, although their missions were well established far before that time. One of the initial goals was to generate interest in the abolition of alcohol, a passion that reached a fevered pitch in 1925 during a revival in the name of future sobriety, an event that stirred a fair amount of controversy. In 1928, the Bourbon Aviation Club was formed, some forty members strong, and promptly sponsored a grand air show that was well received by the locals. The fascination with air travel even inspired the creation of the Bourbon airport in June 1929, but it met with obscurity only a short while later. It is thought that the former airport was situated east of town.

One particular highlight of local history that still carries an aura of heritage was the dedication of the old town pump. A memorial celebration drew great attention and interest on June 30, 1929, as the pump came to symbolize Bourbon's industrious spirit. The memorial, which still stands with pride more than eighty years later, inspired the motif that was adopted for use in the town's flag in 1976. The pump was even designated something of the "guest of honor" during the summertime Town Pump Festival, which was held for many years during the late 1970s and early 1980s. The festival was brought forth through the wiles of the Betsy Ross Club, aptly named during America's bicentennial in 1976. In 1980, the addition of historic homes was launched, with other glimpses into the town's older homes occurring in the late 1990s and early 2000s. The Town Pump Days event was later reworked to include a craft exhibit and sale and is now a two-day affair called the Bourbon Summerfest.

Former mainstays of the Bourbon business panorama dwindled away as the twentieth century moved toward the midway point. The onetime Fribley cider mill, which had been in continuous operation since about 1918, ceased operations and was later sold by 1958. The old Pennsylvania depot, once considered a catalyst for progress and promise, ended service sometime during the early 1950s, with the building itself falling in 1963. Of more uplifting mention, members of Bourbon's oldest lodge, the Masonic #227, transitioned into a generation of greatness with the opening of a new lodge home in 1957, almost one hundred years after

This was one of the first municipal brick buildings created for the improvement of Bourbon services; it served as the town's utility plant. *Larry Lemler.*

the charter was first issued in 1866. The lodge later merged with another area membership, however, and no longer has an auxiliary in Bourbon.

Seven soldiers were taken from the fold of Bourbon's community through the actions of twentieth century war—Max Price, Forrest Weissert and Dale Stine died in World War II; Lamar Troxel and Carl Singery (also recorded as Singrey) were lost in the Korean War; and Richard Peters and Stanley King perished during the Vietnam conflict.

By 1960, the design was formed to allow Bourbon to feature a new three-and-a-half-acre town park, and the site was readied for public use one year later. The recruitment of cutting-edge industry was the mission of the Bourbon Industrial Development Corporation (BIDCO), which was established in 1962. The group spearheaded the efforts and mined the resources to help with the launch of the town's first industrial park, which was developed along the western fringe of the city. With the completion of the U.S. 30 Bypass around the southern edge of town, more growth and more business interest was facilitated.

Also occurring in 1962 was the merging of schools representing the entirety of Bourbon and Bourbon Township, Tippecanoe townships and the students of Etna Township in Kosciusko County. The organization

A wonderfully retro image that captures the carhop era of the 1950s, as seen from the vantage point of Harold Berkeypile's A&W eatery. *Marshall County Historical Museum.*

was originally called the Tri-Township United School Corporation but was later renamed to the Triton School Corporation, the name still in use today. With the securing of the former Bourbon fairgrounds that transpired in 1963, additional plats of land were cobbled onto the original fairground site to permit the construction of new school complex. The Triton Junior-Senior High School opened in 1968, with the first graduates being part of the class of 1969. Tippecanoe and Etna Townships retained separate elementary schools into the early 1970s, until a consolidated elementary school followed in the early 1990s.

The community has had a few of its citizens achieve celebrity status over the past century, starting with the headlines of August 11, 1927, when resident Vern Hazen narrowly missed being struck by a meteor. In the early 1950s, local basketball talent Keith Stackhouse was selected as a "Star of Stars," a title similar to that of Indiana's prestigious "Mr. Basketball" honor. Fast forward to the early 1980s, when Pamela Carlberg achieved placement of third runner-up in the Miss America contest in July 1981, having previously being chosen as both Miss Plymouth and Miss Indiana. Bourbon resident Wendy Rust was another winner in the Indiana Junior Miss Pageant in 1989. The annual World Livestock Auctioneer Championship tournament of 1983 produced another winner with Bourbon ties, Daryl Ball.

Bourbon is presently the residence of about 1,800, where the Triton Trojan pride echoes triumphantly across the graceful farm fields. The Bourbon that is yet to be stands poised on the horizon, and if history serves as any indication, it will certainly include a love for its people and its traditions.

CHAPTER 3
BREMEN

Memoirs from the Marvelous Mint City

It would be difficult to dispute the notion that Bremen carries an ambience as one of northern Indiana's most distinctive small towns. Whether residents from birth, through decision or by fate, many have come to admire the community as a gilded semblance of an idyllic burg, where a foundation of faith remains vibrant along every path and parallel. The well-traversed roadways yield formidable emblems of vitality—businesses have withstood the fickle winds of time and trials, churches have carried messages of hope to the spiritual masses and schools have garnered countless recognition for their pursuit of academia to ensure a promising future for Bremen's youth.

Perhaps every bit as charming is the way it seems you are being cast through a portal of yesteryears simply by wending along the town's periphery. The countryside of rural Bremen captivates residents and travelers alike for its diversity, with the revelation of one of the region's largest Amish populations. Nature and its glories are found at every glance, and there is a peaceful, unassuming manner to the Amish ways that seemingly commands the highest modicum of respect.

However one views the community, through any perspective, Bremen could certainly be considered a land of means and meaning. Or, more succinctly put, in the words of Bremen's longtime official motto, it is above all else "a good town."

Bremen's story begins some 175 years ago, when a small group of travelers, primarily of German descent, descended on northern Marshall County to survey the region and its possibilities for prospective growth. Two gentlemen among those seeking farmlands in and around the area were George Pomeroy and Joseph Geiselman. They decided to establish permanent residency in 1836, christening the future village New Bremen in honor of their beloved homeland across the ocean. New Bremen officially became a part of German Township with the latter's incorporation on May 11, 1838. Of particular interest with regards to the formation of German Township, there was a brief period starting in 1853 when an eastern parcel was carved away from German Township and called Franklin Township. Two years later, though, Franklin Township was dissolved in name, and the land returned to German Township.

By 1846, a post office was launched within the tiny community by David Brothers, who promptly announced that the settlement would be called Brothersville. When George Pomeroy took over the workings of the facility two years later, the name of New Bremen was restored. Within a few more years, near 1851, the town was known simply as Bremen.

Pomeroy was apparently quite a civic-minded fellow, not only taking the reins of the post office but also overseeing the operation of the town's first variety store and serving as a notary public. He served as the lone teacher of Bremen's first public school, a small one-room structure with the meager dimensions of twenty-two feet by thirty feet that was raised in 1853 by Christian Seiler and that doubled in attendance by 1858. This building also produced the first graduating senior class of Bremen High School in 1890, six students strong.

Geiselman, also considered a great contributor to early business, was the force behind the area's first blacksmith shop, which was situated at the southeast corner of Plymouth and Center Streets. He was also the creator of the first frame dwelling within the city limits, which was built in 1850.

George Beyler is the individual who is credited with platting the original boundaries of Bremen prior to its formal designation as a town. In 1851, with incorporation still two decades away, Beyler engineered a layout consisting of forty-eight lots, which encompassed a modest parcel

This is one of the very earliest pictures known to exist of the former downtown square, estimated to have been captured circa 1870. A sign for a livery stable can be seen on the lower level of the white structure on the corner. *Mr. and Mrs. R.T. Henke.*

bordered by Maple Street to the south, Montgomery Street to the west, Bike Street to the north and Center Street to the east. All four of those roadways remain within the downtown sector to this day, all retaining their original names.

Shortly thereafter, others arrived in Bremen and set up shop along and near the heart of the town. In 1854, a sawmill was established on North Center Street by three members of the Ringle family—Daniel Sr., Daniel Jr. and William. Daniel Jr. and his wife, Eliza, were thought to be the parents of the first white child born in Bremen—a daughter named Ellen. One of the Ringle men was also said to be a makeshift pallbearer for one of the first individuals to be buried in Bremen—a man by the name of Youst. Ringle's team of oxen carried the deceased to a piece of land slated for use as a cemetery, with the body readied for burial by placement in a hollowed-out log.

Also transpiring in 1854 was the construction of the first hotel, which was run by the Prottsman (also listed in sources as Protsman) family and was located at the corner of Plymouth and Washington Streets. That is

The Dietrich building and its storefront, as depicted in a vintage postcard from 1911. *From the historical photograph archives of Amy Wenger.*

the legend of statistic, although it is believed that George Pomeroy may have operated an "unofficial" rooming house and saloon during a short time previously. A pharmacist by the last name of Biehl unveiled the first drugstore in 1854, as well, with three additional physicians servicing the township at the same period—Drs. Pollard, Moore and Stange.

The year 1855 marked the origins of what was to become a truly renowned Bremen hallmark for a tenure spanning more than 130 years. J.R. Dietrich founded his first business venture that year at the site where Plymouth and Washington Streets intersect, which at that time served as a makeshift headquarters for a grain milling production that he managed along the North Center Street roadway. By 1873, Dietrich expanded his spectrum of interests to include the operation of a general store, in the city's first brick structure on the southeast corner of Center and Plymouth Streets. The enterprise was immensely successful from its conception, largely in part to its size and stature, allowing for virtually anything to capture a patron's fancy, from clothing to groceries to farm implements.

An expanse of space on the second floor of the Dietrich building became something of a flashpoint for many civic affairs and local government extensions in succeeding years. The first phase of the Bremen State Bank was opened to the public in 1876. Later, the Marquet family operated a tailor shop in that location, and during other intervals, local court proceedings were conducted in the "chambers."

The Dietrich Company, Inc., remained a prominent fixture in the heart of downtown Bremen through several more decades and many more generations of family ownership. The community was rendered shocked and saddened when the announcement was handed down in the fall of 1985 by the remaining Dietrich shareholders and employees that Dietrich's would be closing its doors forever. But what a legacy the family left behind; the bittersweet sentiments having long since waned, it is now much easier to recall the glory years of the Dietrich era. The building itself still stands where it was first raised all those years ago and is now home to a health and fitness complex.

Another longtime establishment that transcended several decades was initiated by the family of John Huff, who first opened a furniture shop and funeral parlor back in 1876. The store was located along the Plymouth Street thoroughfare and remained under the umbrella of generational ownership for almost a century. By the early 1970s, Huff's grandson, Otto, was the store owner, while the funeral home had become a shared venture with the Mishler family.

As the 1860s and 1870s came to pass, more and more businesses were added to Bremen's roster of retail. Christian Schilt and Samuel Schmachtenberger oversaw the bustling Brewer's Mill by 1857, and in 1865, Jacob Knoblock built a new hotel on North Center Street, first called the Thompson House but later known as the Garver House. That building was lost to a fire in 1879. The Wright Bentwood Factory, under the auspices of John J. Wright, was launched in 1869 and within several years' time became the town's largest employer. A. Hadwin, a local machinist, is noted for raising the town's first planing and shingle mill in 1878, but he later sold his interests to William May, who enlarged the business to include machinery repairs and sales. A larger-scale planing and shingle mill following in 1881, led by the duo of Knoepfle and Vollmer, quickly led the region in the distribution of manufactured lumber.

A panoramic glance at the grounds of the former Wright's Bentwood Factory and its workers, seen in this undated photograph. *Mr. and Mrs. R.T. Henke.*

Bremen's status in the region was elevated further with the arrival of the Baltimore and Ohio Railroad in 1874. The addition of the new rail line precipitated the rapid advancement of long-distance communications between neighboring hubs and cities. Telephone service would be provided to the community by 1895, with the main switchboard located at the office of the local newspaper. The Koontz brothers created a separate telephone exchange for Bremen citizens by 1899, later selling its share to the United Telephone Company, which went on serve as the local provider for several more decades.

Newspapers made their debut in Bremen at about the same time as the incorporation took place. The first of these was the *Bremen Clipper*, which was printed by the Macomber brothers for a brief period beginning in 1872. Next came the *Bremen Gazette*, which premiered in 1876 under Charles Sweeney, followed by the *Bremen Banner*, which started its run in 1878, ceased publication for a few years and then resumed for several more years beginning in 1890.

The town's current newspaper is the *Bremen Enquirer*, a weekly assemblage of news and features that was originally called the *Bremen Astonisher* when it was conceived in 1885. It was the brainchild of Brook

When trains passed through Bremen along the Baltimore & Ohio Railroad, this was the point of arrival and departure for countless passengers, some of whom are shown in a picture presumably from the early 1900s. A brick depot was later put into service at the North Center Street station, until it was idled when passenger service was discontinued through the town. The building was in a state of severe disrepair for several decades until it was rescued by the efforts of Historic Bremen, Inc. The group led the charge to restore and renovate the depot to its former glory, and in 2009, it was relocated to the east edge of the SR 106 gateway, where it will be featured as a local visitor's center and museum. *Mr. and Mrs. R.T. Henke.*

Bowman, who later sold it to Samuel Gorrell. Gorrell's son, J.K. Gorrell, later became the managing editor, followed by the James Crittenden family, until the *Enquirer* was corralled into the ownership of the Pilot News organization, based out of Plymouth.

The community's apparent reliance on the lumber industry needed to be evaluated to a great extent with the approach of the twentieth century; many of the trees that supplied the natural inventory for the town's commerce were dwindling in numbers. Agriculture was nudging its way to the forefront of business and livelihood, and early records of the town's existence seem to illustrate this suggestion with a somewhat comical element. It was not uncommon to look outside at any given moment and find cattle, chickens or pigs wandering aimlessly downtown, dodging the horses and buggies that drifted down the dirt roads and

Schlosser's Creamery was another of Bremen's integral, agriculturally based businesses at the turn of the twentieth century, shown here in its prime. The business was started by Henry Schlosser, who was reportedly inspired to go into business by the advent of the mechanical butter churn. Joined by his brother, Philip, Schlosser's Creamery had auxiliary locations in Chicago, Plymouth and Indianapolis during the height of its success. The enterprise remained in the family until it was sold in the 1950s. *Mr. and Mrs. R.T. Henke.*

along the wood-plank sidewalks. Families were extremely self-sufficient in accordance with the farming lifestyle, often canning produce gleaned from their own gardens. Chickens, cows and pigs were staples of the common farmstead, as well. Electricity was an undiscovered novelty, and water had to be dug by hand from primitive wells.

Although Bremen had been in existence for quite some time as a functioning small town, it was at last decided to embrace the legalities of incorporation by 1870. In December of that year, during a session of the Marshall County commissioners, it was ordered to allow the proceedings to move forward, with an election slated to take place among Bremen's residents on January 7, 1871. Thirty-two persons voiced their approval in the matter of incorporation, with no one entering a voice of dissent. Jonas Meiller, Charles Lehr and John Soice, who served as inspectors during the slight but significant election, reported the issue at hand to the commissioners, with the results etched into the permanent court records during the March term of 1871.

The newly minted city (more on this appropriate description later) conducted its first election in May 1871. Bremen was divided into six districts at that time, and a trustee was selected from each. The new board consisted of John Heckerman, Charles Lehr, Christ Hans, John Kuntz, Jacob Walter and Christ Schilt. Lewis Theobald was recruited to serve as clerk-treasurer, David Geyer as the first town marshal and "collector" and Christ Seiler as the assessor. Phillip Keneger was Bremen's first town attorney, and a board of health was installed with a body of two—Drs. Seiler and Younkman.

The council's first agenda dealt with issues considered of tremendous importance relevant to the era. Heckerman, who was chosen to serve as the first board president, led the discussion to implement the town's tax rate—thirty-seven cents for every $100 of assessed valuation on property. Details of the trustee salaries were also ironed out, starting with the town marshal, who earned $50 per year, plus 5 percent of the taxes collected and an additional dollar for every arrest. The assessor would receive $2 per working day, while the clerk-treasurer stood to profit $50 annually, plus 1 percent of garnered tax revenues. Trustees would be paid fifty cents per meeting and slapped with a $3 fine for not being in attendance.

Ordinances drafted on that occasion included: permitting the construction of new wooden sidewalks downtown, working to curtail public intoxication, seeking to abolish littering and prohibiting horse and buggy racing within the town limits. By the end of 1871, the town published a record of financial transaction to date, which included receipts totaling $342.52 and expenses amounting to $321.05.

The final years of the nineteenth century ushered in more change and more growth, both among businesses and residents alike. Another establishment that continues its long and storied tradition ensconced in Bremen's history is Hoople's Tavern, which was opened by Charles Hoople in 1882, directly adjacent to the Dietrich general store. The real estate was procured by Charles Hoople in 1881 for the price of $500. Hoople's son, Ollie, took ownership of the bar by the 1920s, and

Bremen's town hall when first built, during the early twentieth century. The façade was changed over time and replaced with stone, and the building later housed the Bremen State Bank. A major renovation, which ended in 1997, restored the building to its original appearance, and the facility now houses offices of local government, including the chamber of commerce. *Mr. and Mrs. R.T. Henke.*

granddaughter Lucille Hoople Mabbott later carried on as owner until the early 1990s.

The hometown bar and the shenanigans typically fueled by the early atmosphere became part of the inspiration for a nationally syndicated comic strip called *Our Boarding House*, drawn by an artist by the name of Gene Ahern. Ahern was said to be an acquaintance of the Hoople family, and the somewhat embellished stories shared by the Hooples regarding their military service provided additional fodder for the humorous serial, which appeared in many national newspapers in the 1920s and '30s.

Police reports from the closing days of the 1800s reveal that too much imbibing at Hoople's generally led to riotous results. Chronicles of gambling, gunshots in the night air, "gypsy" altercations, prowlers lurking in storefronts, buggy races and other drunken revelries kept the evening patrol rounds lively.

The clientele of Hoople's is decidedly more highbrow than it was in its early years, although some of the traditions long held by the locals have only recently fallen out of favor, such as not allowing women to be seated and served at the bar. Having rightfully secured its place in Hoosier history, Hoople's was honored with the State of Indiana Century Business Award, a recognition given to a longtime business that has maintained ownership within the same family for a century or longer. Hoople's is still very much a fascinating fixture at its original Plymouth Street location, although it is no longer owned by the Hoople family—the family share of the business was sold at auction in 1995.

As Bremen's population soared in the first few years of the 1900s, so did the numbers of schoolchildren. The town's first public school, which had been built on North Montgomery some fifty years prior, had clearly outgrown and outlived its usefulness. Several additions had been tacked on to the original building over the years, and it was becoming apparent that the city needed to modernize to accommodate both the changing face of the community and the advent of a new curriculum.

The public school system had received its charter in 1901, and in the years that followed, the course load was adapted to include such subjects as grammar, history, agriculture, geography and physiology. Attempting to house pupils differing in age and maturity, across a range of grade levels and within a ramshackle collection of old buildings was no longer an acceptable option. Thus began a fervent, five-year-long campaign to generate funds, upon the realization that the old frame structure should be razed and a new brick facility constructed at the same site.

The two-story building was completed in March 1907 at a cost of $40,000 and was warmly received by the townspeople. It was considered to be one of the finest and most beautiful schoolhouses in the county at that time, sporting a red brick exterior, "Bedford stone" trim and hardwood floors. On the upper level, there were four grade rooms, a high school room with two "recitation" nooks, a library, a laboratory and an office for the superintendent. The ground floor featured seven rooms, a wide hallway and an oak-paneled stairway rising to meet the second floor. Every classroom offered a wardrobe for students to store their garments and belongings, and all rooms were well illuminated and adequately heated. Washroom facilities and sinks were located in the basement.

The community's first, stately brick schoolhouse, as it looked at the time of its opening in 1907. *From the historical photograph archives of Amy Wenger.*

Local media reports offered glowing praise for the new school, with one article proclaiming, "He would be a severe critic who could find anything lacking for the comfort, convenience, and satisfaction of the children who will be fortunate enough to use this building."

In 1922, a gymnasium was added to the campus, and this quickly became a tremendous outlet for many community functions, whether they were of an academic nature, sports-themed or purely for entertainment. But there was one major sport that would for many years be missing among the extracurricular activities of the Bremen schools. For a period of time beginning in 1907, there was a passionate outcry from many of the local parents who were outraged over the possibility of their sons participating in what they perceived to be the "barbaric" sport of football. So the sport was removed from the list of electives; it is not known precisely when the sport was reinstated.

For a fair amount of time before and during this particular era, the school calendar resembled nothing of the schedule that students are bound by today. The term was considerably shorter, with the academic year generally commencing in November and reaching completion by March 1. Because Bremen was still very much a farming town, this schedule permitted youngsters to be available to their families during the busiest seasons of the year—the fall harvest and the spring sugar camps. This schedule was typically kept not only by the public school system but also by the smattering of district schools that were still scattered about German Township. That list included the schools of Borkholder, Lozier, Cline, Ridge (also called Huff), Ewald, Wauseon, Willow Grove, Beyler (often called Maple), Mullett, Morning Star, Stuntz, Riverside and Burlington.

In 1936, Bremen's school system was consolidated with that of rural German Township, a move that warranted the construction of a new school building, unveiled in 1939 with a price tag of $250,000. The funds were secured in part by a federal Public Works Administration grant, with the rest financed through a local bond issue. The dual-level building, still part of the current campus, housed the primary and middle school grades along the lower floor, while the majority of the upper classrooms were dedicated to the high school students. Minor additions were implemented during the 1950s, with a separate high school building finally being created in 1962. A major renovation transpired in 1978 with the addition of a swimming pool and an auditorium at the high school, and another large reworking of the grounds occurred in 1989, when the "link" was built to connect the two buildings, creating more classroom space and a new gymnasium that would replace the old elementary school gym.

Bremen also has one private learning institution, St. Paul's Lutheran School, whose origins in the community reach back to 1846. Reverend G.K. Schuster organized the first school of the Lutheran denomination, and at that time, classes were held within the existing church. A separate school was later built by 1858 at 218 North Washington Street, and the school would be expanded and relocated several more times in later years. In time, the Lutheran School would have a modest campus at 220 East Maple Street, followed by its inclusion near the Lutheran church at 214 East South Street. The school and its sponsoring church are now both situated in the 600 Block of South Center Street.

During those very early years of the 1900s, Bremen's population nearly doubled in size, swelling from 1,000 citizens to nearly 1,700. Those numbers are attributed to the increase of employment opportunities that

Bremen Public Schools, as it appeared during its unveiling in 1939. The facility presently houses students in the elementary and middle school grades, and a separate high school building, opened in 1961, is located just south of the original school. *From the historical photograph archives of Amy Wenger.*

drew families from across the nation to seek out the northeast sector of Marshall County for residence. The community's largest and most widely regarded employer at that time was the Holland Radiator Company, which was later called the American Radiator Company, or simply, ARCO. It was the frontrunner in the production of heating elements and equipment and was one of the first manufacturers in the area to unionize workers in 1901.

Also taking place in the name of modern convenience was the upgrading of municipal utilities such as water, electricity and sewer systems, occurring at a seemingly furious pace. Only a few years prior, a water storage standpipe had been erected and subsequently dedicated, ideally poised to handle the needs of the community. Built at a cost of about $8,000, the suggestion to design such a tower did not initially meet with a favorable reception, as some residents voiced concerns over the terrific expense. The tide of public opinion shifted drastically, though, when a massive fire nearly erased an entire block of the Plymouth Street corridor.

An old view taken from the North Jackson Street neighborhood vantage point, where the Wright Opera House can be seen on the corner and just into the distance, the historic water standpipe. This perspective remains relatively intact today, with only minor changes along the building façades—as well as, of course, a paved road. *Mr. and Mrs. R.T. Henke.*

So the project forged on, with a tank created using thirty-six feet of steel plates riveted at six-foot intervals, the end result equipped to hold thirty thousand gallons of water. The storage tank was then perched atop a towering brick base standing sixty-eight feet in height. An iron guardrail crowned the uppermost part of the tower, and an interior stairwell allowed workers to maneuver the equipment when necessary. The standpipe, which remained in service until 1956, was declared to be an American Historical Landmark in August 1975 by the American Water Works and remains one of the only structures of its kind to be found in the nation.

Little is known or recorded as to how the first network of underground sewers came into being. There are indications that by 1902 a drainage system was installed along North Center Street, not far from the railroad tracks. As further units were added, they were outfitted for runoff into either the Armey Ditch or the Yellow River.

The source of electrical services was centralized to a series of town-owned generators, working within a powerhouse, where Shadyside Park now stands. All of the boilers and generators were working concurrently with the water pumps. The main downtown thoroughfares were now being lit through a grid of thirty-two "arc" lights.

Unfortunately, with this additional boost of illumination during the evening hours, the setting allowed a certain sense of debauchery to prevail. An editorial in a 1908 edition of the *Bremen Enquirer* groused, "Public drunkedness, profanity, gambling, and general rowdyism are all lending to the sentiment that the town's six saloons must go." In a defeat for the cause of crime prevention, however, the governing bodies of both Bremen and German Township opted to allow their region to remain "wet," while the surrounding portions of the county chose to "go dry."

By this time, the folks of Bremen were ably suited to enjoy times of recreation as well as the perseverance of honest work. Many clubs and organizations were experiencing surges in membership on account of the higher numbers of residents. Active civic groups included the Bremen Masonic Lodge #414, Free and Accepted Masons, the Order of the Eastern Star, Chapter No. 117; the Knights and Sisters of Pythias; and

One of the truly hidden treasures of downtown—in that it literally was tucked away beneath the Plymouth Street commercial block—this was a local bowling alley, seen in this 1908 image, that was accessed through a ground-level entrance near Hoople's Tavern. *Mr. and Mrs. R.T. Henke.*

Not many children seemed willing to wait for a turn on this attraction at Bremen's first town park, called Shadyside, located on North Center Street just beyond the railroad. *Mr. and Mrs. R.T. Henke.*

the Current Events Club. Also, the National Women's Relief Corps Auxiliary to the Grand Army of the Republic chartered an offshoot branch that it called the Hartzog Post of the Women's Relief Corps. The club was later renamed the Herzog Post in honor of Christian Herzog, who was one of Bremen's first casualties during World War I.

Other resources that enhanced cultural awareness came in the form of the Ciceronian Literary Society and many traveling Chautauqua performers, who often appeared at the Wright Opera House bringing their literary and musical talents to showcase. Revivals, Sunday school gatherings and Bible study groups were also frequently encouraged. Many musical extravaganzas presented by the town bands also brought sound and spectacle to the downtown square.

Meanwhile, as the people of Bremen were practicing their strong work ethics and reveling in their community spirit, a young farmer quietly drifted into town and would forever change the perception of Bremen's business environment. William Leman Sr. arrived in Marshall County by way of central Illinois by 1911 with the hopes of creating a peppermint and spearmint farm. This was during a time when mint crops were a fairly common commodity for the region. In the years following 1914,

One of many mint stills that were strewn about northern Marshall County—more than likely a supplier to the William Leman mint oil refinery that was launched in the early twentieth century. *From the historical photograph archives of Amy Wenger.*

Leman broadened his scope of expertise to include a mint oil processing facility, accomplished by developing a rapport with area mint farmers and purchasing their crops for use in the making of oil. Leman's dream of opening a local mint oil refinery was finally realized, guided and led for many more decades by several generations of sons, brothers, nephews and other family members.

Because the company was able to achieve international prominence in both the unique nature of its genre and its admirable reputation, Bremen would henceforth be christened the "Mint City." Several area businesses would also incorporate the allusion to mint in their company names, such as the Sprig O' Mint golf course, Mint City Motors auto sales and the Mint City Villas; the Bremen High School yearbook was known affectionately for many years as the "Sprig." It was not uncommon to tarry around Bremen during daylight hours and be greeted by the wafting scent of peppermint lingering in the air.

When the Veterans of Foreign Wars announced the formation of its local chapter, #8972, by the late 1940s, William and four of his brothers—Nelson, John, Samuel and Ardale—were among the very first members inducted.

Several members of the Leman family were also among those collectively chosen to receive one of the community's first Lifetime Achievement Awards in 1998. One of the most beloved and enduring creations of William Leman, Inc., was the "Leman mint," a peppermint candy that came in two styles, "button" and "football." The candies are still a staple of local merchants, although they are now being distributed and produced by Atkinson Candy Company of Lufkin, Texas, having previously been crafted by longtime candy maker Peerless Candy of Chicago.

The 1920s saw a larger influx of the "infernal machine" along Bremen's cobblestone and dirt roadways, which would be paved with brick by 1913 to ease the transition to motor vehicles. Automobiles, while not exactly a rarity at that time, were somewhat of a novelty alongside the rural mannerisms of the community. By a rather eerily prescient stroke of coincidence, that was the same year that the Don-Durant-Lichtenberger

In this scene from 1914, which corresponds to the dates barely distinguishable on the license plates, a handful of gentlemen appear eager to flaunt their flivvers while posing for a photograph, as a sales banner for Ponader's Grocery provides an interesting backdrop. *Mr. and Mrs. R.T. Henke.*

livery stable, one of the earliest businesses in town, burned entirely to the ground. The event was viewed by many locals as a symbolic conclusion to the age of the horse-drawn carriage.

Bremen's first automobile dealership was the J.W. Brougher agency, the local distributor of Buick cars—"the Ideal Car for every man and within reach of all, a wonderful car celebrated for style, fine finish, and durability of engine." With the increasing number of automobiles motoring about town, people had to become increasingly mindful of the speeds possessed by the newfangled machines, and there was a steep uptick in car-pedestrian accidents noted for a time. Local doctors also wryly commented on the increasing number of injuries they called "Ford fractures," caused by overzealous cranking of engines. The cars would oftentimes kick violently upward, snapping men's arms at the wrists like fragile twigs.

On the subject of medicine, although there were plenty of physicians abounding as far back as the town's infancy, there were always hopes that Bremen could accommodate a local hospital. In the late 1800s and early 1900s, the town was not immune, so to speak, in sometimes being bewitched by any number of traveling "doctors" who offered cures for virtually every ache and affliction. Newspapers were casting their opinions as to whether the town would be within its powers to found the Community Hospital, and meanwhile naïve townsfolk occasionally relied on any number of patent tonics, syrups, powders and salves, seeking relief from whatever ailed them.

During one particular noteworthy event, the entire general population was quarantined under a cloud of fear and panic in 1907, beginning during the graduation exercises at the public school. Apparently, one of the graduates was severely stricken with smallpox, though this was unknown at the time. Because virtually everyone residing in Bremen and the surrounding region was in attendance for this occasion, a sweeping order was later executed commanding that everyone stay indoors until the worst of the infections had subsided. It was not recorded exactly how many individuals were exposed and later fell ill during the weeks that followed.

It was in 1943 that the first glimpses were revealed of what would become Bremen's first hospital. That year, Mr. and Mrs. William Myers purchased a house on the corner of South Whitlock and West Grant Streets and transformed it into a convalescent home. The Myers family continued with that operation for about three years, when the Church of the Brethren joined ownership of the facility. The first steps were taken to add other facets of service to the complex, including the addition of a maternity ward, something that Mrs. Myers very much wanted to see come about. She never lived to see her dream carried out, however—she perished in a car accident in 1946.

About 1948, the church expressed an interest in seeing the hospital grow to meet the rising demand of the most current medical services, but members were worried that the enterprise was becoming too large of an entity for them to continue managing. The governing trustees decided to put the issue before a public forum to gauge the community's interest in allowing the hospital to reign under the ownership of

The first Community Hospital of Bremen first opened as a convalescent home in 1943 and was later governed by German Township trustees and residents in 1948. This was the hospital that served the people of Bremen for almost sixty years until the arrival of a modern medical complex just a few years later. Today, the original hospital still stands, under the ownership of Doctor's Hospital of Bremen, and includes a host of outpatient rehabilitation offerings. The white house in the background has since been removed to make way for additional parking. *From the historical photograph archives of Amy Wenger.*

German Township. Residents willingly backed the endeavor and voiced no opposition to the collection of donations and a tax levy of five cents for the purpose of securing public funding. Within the span of just one year, the necessary monies were accrued and the Community Hospital of Bremen was incorporated.

The hospital was enlarged further in 1957 to allow for the inclusion of all basic aspects of hospital service, including the long-desired maternity wing. Over time, other amenities were offered, including twenty-four-hour emergency care, a laboratory, ambulatory surgery, occupational medicine and physical therapy, radiology and home health assistance. Community Hospital of Bremen was Indiana's first to be designated a "Critical Access Hospital," in 1999.

With the addition of such a wide variety of services, though, came the realization that the older building was not quite streamlined or updated enough for so many provisions, and so discussions began to circulate about the possibility of a new hospital. The enormous success of a fundraising drive, during which one individual sent a check for $100,000, along with the approval of several federally backed grants and loans, preceded a groundbreaking ceremony for the proposed new site on October 22, 2004. Community Hospital of Bremen is now a single-story, multimillion-dollar medical complex that sprawls along the horizon of a tranquil countryside setting on the northernmost edge of Bremen, along State Road 331. It was officially opened to the public in 2006.

By the midway point of the twentieth century, industry was rapidly taking center stage as a leading source of both jobs and revenue. One of the frontrunners that consistently captured headlines with news of progress, expansions and employment opportunities was Liberty Coach, which was the first business to anchor an industrial park on the city's west side. A second industrial sector was created in 1964 and featured several long-running establishments, including Bremen Builders, Universal Bearings, Ristance Wire, the Corl Corporation, Bornemann Products and TV Time Foods.

One of those premier institutions that retains a prominent place in the northeast industrial corridor is Bremen Castings, Inc., which originated in 1939 as the Bremen Gray Iron Foundry. Launched by a local trio of

Bremen's fire department was formerly housed in this building along South Center Street and is shown here circa the 1940s with a fleet of three fire trucks, a tanker, an emergency vehicle and a boat. Today, this is the headquarters for the Bremen Police Department, while the firefighters have a separate building adjacent to this one, on West South Street. *From the historical photograph archives of Amy Wenger.*

men, Ellis Brown, Harold Heckamen and Charles W. King, the company has earned a formidable reputation nationwide as a source for parts and materials used in farm machinery, pipe fittings, lawn and garden implements, engines and valves, to list a few. Several generations of the Brown family have retained principal interest and leadership for Bremen Castings since its debut more than sixty years ago.

The first official string of storefronts to be billed as a shopping center was opened in 1951, under the guidance of Kenney Gilbert, who for the previous ten years had been the proprietor of the local grocery store he called Kenney's Kash and Karry. Gilbert moved his grocery to the new plaza, which later featured a wealth of small but esteemed businesses whose names still come up in conversation among local reminiscences, though their existence has since faded. Longtime locals surely remember partaking of meals at the Kopper Kettle, shopping for children's apparel at Tot 'n' Teen Togs or purchasing groceries at Kenney's Super Foods. Gilbert's name tops the list of inductees into the chamber of commerce's

Lifetime Achievement honorarium, being one of the very first to be chosen in 1997.

Gilbert's friendly rival in the affections of local grocery shoppers was Woodrow Schramm, who initially operated his store as an IGA franchise in 1943. The store that bears his name, called simply Woodie's Supermarket, is now Bremen's lone supermarket, and the man who inspired it lent his many talents to a number of local causes over the years. He and his wife were instrumental in the creation of the Woodie's Scholarship fund, which still grants monetary awards to college-bound individuals, and a winding road in the southeast niche of Bremen is known as Woodie's Lane.

Another longtime business that for decades has created generations of warm memories for Bremen folks is the Wooden Peel, the town's atmospheric and trademark pizza parlor. John and Sandy Sullivan were the first pair to oversee the operation, followed by a two-year ownership by Bill and Rita Leeper. Chuck and Carol Beutel bought the business in 1981, and the ownership has remained within the Beutel family ever since, currently under the coordination of Kathy Beutel-Galloway. The "Peel" was always the landing spot following and preceding all sporting events starring the Bremen Lions, school dances and virtually any other occasion that happened to call for a gathering. Pizza, pasta and other entrees are so sought after by both those who still reside in Bremen and those who have moved elsewhere that it is now possible to send a "virtual pizza" from the Peel on the social network website Facebook.

The year 2010 marks the sixtieth anniversary of Bremen's largest and most visited annual affair, the Firemen's Festival. The jovial sounds of the carnival atmosphere have been a summertime sensation for the community since its creation in 1950. The event is typically held during the first week of July and ends with a spectacular fireworks display. Animal exhibits, commercial displays, dozens of food booths, games and other features draw tens of thousands of guests to Bremen. Luehr's Ideal Rides has been the longtime provider of the carnival, offering its extensive variety of rides since the 1960s.

Perhaps the most splendid way to close this chapter of the Mint City history is to offer a tribute to one of the community's most respected and lauded citizens, Dr. Otis R. Bowen. Bowen and his young family arrived in Bremen in the spring of 1946 at the start of his longtime career as a local physician. Regarded by Marshall County residents to be one of the most beloved family doctors of his time, more than one generation of Bremenites can lay claim to being a "Bowen baby."

In the 1950s, Bowen's congenial nature and devotion to the issues of his new hometown were the impetus for his entrance into the political realm. In the fall of 1952, Bowen handily defeated his opponent in a race for the office of county coroner. Bowen's next venture was to capture a seat in the Indiana House of Representatives, which he obtained by wagering a modest and fair campaign and electing to focus on what he could offer to his constituents, rather than practicing vindictive tactics. Bowen maintained his position within the House for more than a decade, from 1956 until 1970, with six years of service as Speaker of the House.

By the late 1960s, motivated by the enthusiasm of his many comrades in politics, as well as his friends and family of Bremen, Bowen actively pursued the office of governor, although he was defeated during his first bid in 1968. Undaunted, Bowen pledged to make another run for the 1972 election and promptly set about the task of developing his platform. Although he did not officially declare his candidacy until 1971, by then he had already won the affections of legions of followers both local and beyond. Bowen himself later recalled of this particular time spent mingling among supporters that he had shaken hands so often that the fingers of his right hand took on a perpetually painful and swollen state.

Bowen was the victor in a thrilling state election held in early November 1972 and took his place as the forty-fourth governor of Indiana for the next eight years, encompassing two terms between 1973 and 1981. Bowen's name also reached national recognition in the mid-1980s, when he was selected by then president Ronald Reagan to serve as the sixteenth secretary of health and human services. He remained in that post from 1985 until 1989.

Bowen is peacefully living his golden years in the community in which his political, personal and professional aspirations all came to light.

CHAPTER 4

CULVER

A Grand Institution on the Shores of Lake Maxinkuckee

The eloquence and beauty along the shores of Lake Maxinkuckee, and that surrounds the haven of Culver, has lingered in the dreams of many a poet, composer and author in various moments across time. Impressions of the graceful tranquilities have been immortalized in passages of poetry, melodies of music and volumes of verse.

Surprisingly, one might consider a place of such wistful inspiration to have maintained a singular title of reference among records of history, but Culver has only been named as such for about sixty years. The century preceding the christening of Culver saw many name changes, all transpiring through intriguing circumstances.

A map depicting the Marshall County region, dating back to 1843, reveals that the first name of the tiny settlement in Union Township was Geneva. For a short time following, it was referred to as the Yellow River Post Office. Then, in 1844, a gentleman named Bayless L. Dickson purchased farmland bordering on Lake Maxinkuckee and set about laying and platting the region for settlement. The certificate, filed on June 8, 1844, listed the new village as Union Town.

Several years later, a fellow of French descent, Dr. G.A. Durr, arrived in town and petitioned a new name for Union City, which was then undergoing a massive resurveying effort. In 1851, Durr was successful in his campaign to call the town Marmont (or Marmount, as noted in some records), in recognition of a respected French general of the same name. So Marmont it remained for the next forty-two years, and it continued to be called by that time when it was incorporated in 1894.

At the time of its organization, Marmont had been a fairly new place of residence for the man who would, without question, become one of the greatest leaders of Culver's storied past. Henry Harrison Culver arrived from Ohio in 1883, seeking a quiet place to recover from illness. Culver was a man of enormous clout and wealth, which was matched equally by the generosity he extended to the town that he held in such high regard. Culver was an activist on a number of local fronts, one of his early endeavors being the donation of land for the purpose of an annual fair.

But nowhere are Culver's contributions more evident than in the preparatory boarding school that bears his name. The Culver Military Academy was founded in 1894 "for the purpose of thoroughly preparing young men for the best colleges, scientific schools, and businesses of America."

A view of the marching battalion of the Culver Military Academy during its early days. *Marshall County Historical Museum.*

Two years after its unveiling, the population of CMA rose on account of a fire at the Missouri Military Academy, an event that prompted a consolidation with Culver. Missouri's headmaster, Colonel Alexander Fleet, took over the leadership of the academy and was largely instrumental in its rapid growth in the early twentieth century. Another early force in securing CMA's prestigious reputation was General Leigh Gignilliat, who was at the helm of the academy beginning in 1939. By 1971, the Culver Girls' Academy was opened, and in the nearly forty years since, the campus of the Culver Academies has captured world renown and distinction in academics and athletics, with students enrolled from across the United States and around the globe.

In celebration of Culver's civic-mindfulness and devotion, the county's board of commissioners accepted a proposal to call the community Culver City. The vote took place on October 4, 1895, with no one casting a negative vote. The visionary for whom Culver will always be remembered passed away two years after his honor, his death occurring on September 26, 1897.

The story did not end there, however, because when the name was presented to the federal postal authorities in Washington, the commissioners were informed that there was already a town called Culver. Interestingly enough, the "first" Culver was not far from the newly revised one—it was located in nearby Tippecanoe County. So the petition was thereby denied.

Through the financial and persuasive intervention of Henry H. Culver, though, the matter would be resolved. Culver traveled to Tippecanoe County and discovered that their Culver was named for a man named Crane Culver. Culver offered to take on all of the legal and monetary expenses that would be incurred by submitting to a name change and convinced the town to reinvent itself as Crane. Once the powers in Washington were made aware of the legalities of the name transfer, the Town of Culver was reinstituted in Marshall County, and was officially listed as such. The "Town of" portion was later dropped in 1949, leaving behind simply the name of Culver.

By the arrival of the twentieth century, Culver's population had risen to just over five hundred citizens. For the next few years, newcomers were

Main Street in downtown Culver, as it looked in the early twentieth century. *Marshall County Historical Museum.*

drawn to the practicality and the beauty of the shoreline along Lake Maxinkuckee, and so development near the waterfront rose dramatically during the first two decades, with the town of Culver itself maintaining a steady number of residents.

Lake Maxinkuckee, today known as the second-largest natural lake in the state of Indiana, was a region of great importance during the days of the Potawatomi Indians. Surrounded by several acres of forest and visited by wildlife of varying species, the lake itself measured about three miles in length and more than two miles across at its widest point. At the time of Marshall County's organization in 1836, the land was inhabited by three separate Indian reservations, all bordering the east side of the lake.

One reservation belonged to the people of Chief Neeswaugee, whose settlement came near to where Henry Harrison Culver eventually took residence. The people of Chief Quashqua's tribe composed the population of the reservation situated in the middle. The Aubenaube reservation was the one aligned farthest south and was of such vast dimension as to extend a considerable distance into adjacent Fulton County.

The name "Maxinkuckee" is not, in its present form, considered to be of true Indian translation but was certainly inspired from American Indian culture. As was likely expected with a lake bearing such a complicated moniker, there were many misspellings recorded at various intervals. Poor penmanship possibly led to one early misconstrued record—in field notes taken by a state auditor during the late nineteenth century, the word was written to appear as "Mekinkeekee." More than one individual, however, misread the notes on account of the scrawled handwriting, as indicated by the records of the state, which listed the lake as "Maxinkuckee." Furthermore, the translation given at the federal level calls the lake "Muksencucku." The discrepancy was blamed on varying brushstrokes by the use of quill pens, with many of the vowels unintentionally taking on the appearance of other letters.

But Maxinkuckee was the version that remained, yet even its meaning continues to have an aura of mystique. The word is said to have syllables gleaned from other countries, with "Max" being a German word and the balance of the word taking origins from Scotch, Irish, American and Algonquin Indian influences. One early settler in the Lake Maxinkuckee area, a fellow by the name of Charles Cook, was said to have had congenial relations with the Potawatomis still in residence, and he was told that the name of the lake came from the Indian word for "moccasin," meaning that the American Indians believed the lake to be shaped as such.

Another account relays a translation offered by Simon Pokagon, the last of the Potawatomi chiefs to reside in the Midwest. In response to an inquiry by a local historian, Pokagon shared that the term "Maxinkuckee" loosely came from the Indian phrase meaning "there is grass." Still another story indicates that the name is derived from the declaration that the lake provided "clear blue water."

So it would seem that there is no one right way to consider the source of the name, for they are both essentially true, then as now.

Lake Maxinkuckee spawned a small village bearing its name in the latter part of the 1800s, which was located about half a mile east of the lake itself. The little town was of meager proportions during the fairly short duration it was of significance. There was a brick schoolhouse, which was built in 1908 and later became a cold storage facility for apples,

Swimmers abound in and around Lake Maxinkuckee, seen in this circa 1920s image. *Marshall County Historical Museum.*

run by the Bigley family. The building achieved prominence as a county historical landmark in 1983. Members of the Bigley family were some of the first white settlers to reside in this particular area and maintained a family farmstead dating back to 1844 that was later passed to several succeeding generations. The property was bestowed with a Hoosier Homestead Award for keeping ownership within the same family for more than a century.

The burg also featured a general store owned by Eli Parker and John Wise, later taken over by Anson Overmyer. The Allegheny House, which was also designated a county landmark in 1983, was once the site of a tavern and inn, and was built in 1855. The Methodist Protestant Church, with a cornerstone inscribed with the date 1888, was also located near the town, at the north side of 18B Road. The largest store in town was a two-story brick structure, raised in 1907 by the Bigley brothers, Guy and Chester. The duo operated a meat market, a grocery store and an ice cream parlor on the lower level and also sold gasoline and kerosene. Living rooms were located upstairs, with two rooms in the rear housing the local telephone company. Water was provided to the building by way of a flowing well, which was siphoned through a large wheel attached to the side of the building. The store complex was razed in 1969, but the church was salvaged, first in use as a retirement facility and later converted into a private residence.

As Lake Maxinkuckee and its environs were quietly maintaining its tranquility and charm, the town of Culver was eyeing avenues for future growth and expansion. Realizing that more buildings would certainly merit better means to ensure their safety, Culver installed its first community fire department in 1903. The unit was a rather small one and utilized only the most basic methods of extinguishing fires, in a manner typically referred to as "bucket brigades."

In the spring of 1906, a fundraising drive was launched to persuade the community that more adequate fire protection was needed, particularly in light of the building boom that had just sprung forth downtown. The situation was illustrated in stark, tragic form that summer, when two devastating fires occurred. The first one decimated a new $50,000 gymnasium at the Culver Military Academy, while the second wiped out a series of ice storage facilities on the south side of Culver. The icehouses were quickly rebuilt, as the harvesting of ice along Lake Maxinkuckee was imperative to the town's infrastructure during the frigid winter months.

Meanwhile, as Culver was working to strengthen its standing as a vibrant small city, the people were also keenly aware of maintaining the image it was projecting as a something of a safe harbor for visitors. Interesting statutes were issued in the first few years of the 1900s, such as the execution of a ten-dollar fine to anyone caught hitching their horses to the picturesque shade trees. Naturally, this led to the town council sheepishly admitting that perhaps there should be money set aside to build more hitching posts in town. Another topic of discussion centered on the need to have a decent "public bath" in town, while a 1908 law stipulated that "gas buggies" were permitted to drive at speeds not to exceed eight miles per hour. Young lads from the Culver Military Academy were oftentimes hired for a wage of fifty cents per day, their primary task being the removal of dandelions about campus and the nearby lakeshore. And in 1905, a graceful gliding water vehicle debuted called the *White Swan Pavilion*. The recreational boat was designed to

Lake Maxinkuckee's Floating Pavilion glides gracefully on the water during its heyday in the 1910s. *Marshall County Historical Museum.*

entice passengers and residents alike with the promise of spectacular views, music and dancing.

To further facilitate Culver's increasing local population, a new school building was opened in 1906. Franklin Overmyer paid $12,000 for the construction of the school, and he in turn rented it to the board of trustees for public use. Several lots nearby, where the former schoolhouse had been, were sold off, with the largest lot going to John Osborn. Osborn used part of the former school structure and added improvements to the structure, converting the facility into a hotel.

Also taking place in 1906 was the creation of the town waterworks, which was considered a major improvement necessary for Culver's continued growth. New buildings for the bank and the post office came along in 1907, which was also a banner year for the ice harvesters, hauling in an astronomical load of forty thousand tons of ice. It was said that the workers were paid for their hard laboring with gold from the local bank. Culver's first electric sign appeared in 1908 along the façade of the Saine store, and a new golf course was opened to sports enthusiasts at the east side of the lake.

Other newsworthy events that were observed included the formation of the Culver City Club in 1911, an organization launched by the

The famed Black Horse Troop of Culver Military Academy, which was featured in a circa 1920s documentary detailing points of interest in northern Indiana. *Marshall County Historical Museum.*

women of the town. By 1912, the *White Swan Pavilion* would be retired and replaced by the Floating Pavilion. News accounts boast of a three-story "skyscraper" about to begin construction in 1913 in the business sector. And in one unconfirmed account of a phenomenal sports contest, it was said that Culver High School basketball standout Herman Sayger managed to singularly rack up 113 points during a March 8, 1913 meeting against Winamac. Needless to say, Culver was victorious, with the final score said to be Culver 154, Winamac 10.

During the ten-year span covering 1910 to 1920, Culver was singled out for recognition as being the community with the greatest amount of growth. Even so, Culver continued to capture headlines from time to time, and not necessarily for laudable reasons. During the final months of World War I, the national coal shortage struck the town with particular ferocity. Many public buildings, including the well-patronized saloons, restaurants and theatres that drew residents and tourists alike, had to be temporarily closed. Over on Lake Maxinkuckee, complaints began pouring in over the latest trend in women's swimwear: the one-piece skirted suit. And just days before Christmas in 1920, a bank robbery carried out by a quintet of criminals resulted in severe injury to Jerome Zechiel and the death of A.R. Saine, both prominent Culver citizens. Enraged vigilantes gave chase to the throng of bandits, with four of the five apprehended—the fifth individual was never caught.

In 1923, the Ku Klux Klan made an appearance in the area, presumably to create some type of recruitment attempt. While other, smaller factions were said to be gathering elsewhere in the county, much had been left out of the records of history, due to the questionable nature of the organization.

Not all of the news was lacking in optimism, though. Many milestones were coming about during the '20s and '30s, such as the inclusion of mail service in 1925 and the opening of the town's first airport in 1928. In the late 1920s, the Culver Military Academy became the set for a feature film, called *Prep and Pep*, with the campus radio station premiering at about the same time, with the call letters WCMA. One of Culver's key thoroughfares connecting Culver and Plymouth was slated for paving in 1928, later named Olive Trail. The former Culver-Logansport Road followed in 1934, now known as State Road 17.

Culver's residents were thrilled to learn of the purchase of forty boulevard lights that had been showcased at the Chicago World's Fair in 1933. The lights were installed in the town square, with some later moved to the town park. A new post office came under construction by 1935, with a new mural by Indianapolis artist Mrs. Hendrick Mayer unveiled in 1938, entitled *The Arrival of Mail*.

The national spotlight turned back to Culver Military Academy in the late 1930s when some of the biggest actors in Hollywood arrived there to film a movie called *The Spirit of Culver*. The roster of stars included Jackie Cooper, Eddie Bartholomew, Andy Devine and Tim Holt, who was a CMA graduate.

By the end of the 1930s and early 1940s, the specter of World War II loomed ominously over the nation, and Culver residents were not exempt from the perilous sentiments. In all, the community lost nineteen servicemen to the battles, beginning on December 7, 1941, with the Japanese attack on Pearl Harbor. Patrick Finney was the town's first

This picture postcard from about the turn of the twentieth century shows people strolling about the scenic campus of the Culver Military Academy. *Marshall County Historical Museum.*

casualty, perishing on that fatefully historic day. Culver's chapter of the Veterans of Foreign Wars was organized shortly after the conclusion of the war, in 1946. The first soldier to lose his life following the VFW charter was Robert Hickman, a soldier of the Korean War.

The residents of the town were surely seeking refuge from the atrocities occurring across the seas, so the community set out to provide positive outlets to which their people could look. The Culver Lions' Club was instituted in 1943, and shortly thereafter, the members sponsored a lavish regatta on Lake Maxinkuckee, providing entertainment to enthusiastic audiences. Enraptured crowds also turned out to see the occasional moonlight serenade at the lake, which featured selections by the CMA band. A naval school boat provided a beautiful twilight backdrop for the band's stage as the music drifted across the night air. The much-loved affair continued to be a summer tradition for many decades to follow.

The Culver High School basketball team of 1944 was seemingly an answer to prayer, offering fans a thrilling season of twenty-eight consecutive wins—an accomplishment that rendered the squad the best in the state. The lads were known as the "Whiz Kids" and experienced no difficulty taking the regional title, but they later lost a heartbreaking matchup at the state level, losing to the boys of LaPorte. Many Culver residents sacrificed gasoline and tires—a luxury to many during the days of rationing—to be able to travel away from Culver to cheer on their victorious team.

Several noteworthy events marked the passing of the 1950s, including a 1952 report indicating that many residents passionately claimed to have viewed "flying saucers" in the sky over Lake Maxinkuckee—a sensational story that swept through the excited community. The Culver movie house reached national prominence in 1954, with its distinction of being the smallest movie house in America to install cinemascope. The first motion picture that was shown with the breakthrough method was *The Robe*. Also that year, the end of one era and the beginning of another came after a local hotel ended an eighty-two-year reign of recognition as the Maxinkuckee Inn. The new name was, simply, the Culver Inn.

A new school was under construction, utility upgrades were taking place, the telephone company was adapting to change and a new gas

The Maxinkuckee Inn, perched along the shoreline of Lake Maxinkuckee, as depicted in this undated photo. *Marshall County Historical Museum.*

company was preparing to open as the decade drew to a close. The academy was featured in a 1959 *Life* magazine piece, in which the article described the christening of Admiral Yarnell and several related activities revolving around the Independence Day observance.

Reorganizing the boundaries of the school districts was a leading priority by 1960, with discussions resulting in the consolidation of Culver, Aubenaubee Township in Fulton County and North Bend Township in Starke County. A land option for a new high school was pursued by 1964, with a new high school at last ready for use by 1968. Also taking place in 1960 was the crowning of a Culver celebrity, the singer Miss Tommye Lou Glaze. Glaze was the talent contest winner for the Miss Plymouth and Miss Indiana Pageants who then went on to compete at the Miss America competition, bringing home a fourth-place finish.

As the tumultuous 1960s marched on and the 1970s dawned, there were highs and lows taking place locally as well. The McGill Manufacturing Company began operations in 1965, bringing about brisk business and employment opportunities. It remained a fixture of Culver commerce for another twenty years, until a 1985 strike, coupled with the effects of a recession, led to the permanent shuttering of the facility. In 1967, the Crabb Furniture Store ended its run in the community after fifty-four years of service.

One of Culver's most gifted artisans became the recipient of the Indiana Sesquicentennial Medal in 1973. Known as a "Culver's Star Artist," Warner Williams was an artist in residence of the Culver Academy. He came to the area in 1940 by way of Henderson, Kentucky, where he was born in 1903. He was widely renowned and respected for his medal designs and sculptures, many of which are on display at the Culver Public Library. Williams designed the fiftieth anniversary medallion for the Indianapolis Speedway and also created a logo for the state's sesquicentennial celebration. Williams died in September 1982.

In the 1970s, Culver was the recipient of a substantial federal grant in excess of $260,000 to revive and renovate the public beach house and surrounding shores of Lake Maxinkuckee. The former Culver Hotel was renamed once again, this time dedicated as the Osborn Center in a nod to the civic contributions of William O. Osborn. The event was touted as being of relevance to senior citizens, as the building was being revamped for their use as a social facility.

A local historian by the name of Robert Rust once made an astute observation regarding the people of this region. "Culver is a town of three divisions—townies, the permanent residents; lake people, who come for the summer; academy people and students, whose permanent home for some is Culver and for others, a school term residence only." That statement still carries sound merits today.

More than 150 years ago, there were inklings that the Culver area would become something of great importance, as was noted in a news brief from the *Marshall County Republican*, dated February 15, 1858: "A meeting will be held at the schoolhouse in Union Town to take into consideration the propriety of forming a society, to be known as the 'Antiquarian and Historical Society,' for the purpose of collecting as many of the circumstances and incidents relative to the settlement of this region of the country, from the first settlement to the present time, that may be read for posterity, which we believe will be of great interest." It is now the mission of the present-day Culver Antiquarian and Historical Society to preserve, respect and honor the moments that have come from all facets and walks of Culver life to create the most fascinating blended history, which it now treasures with pride.

CHAPTER 5

PLYMOUTH

Of Pilgrims and Pioneers—the Homeland of the Rockies

Without question, of all the great cities and towns within Marshall County, the story of how Plymouth came into being is one of the most fascinating. It is a city that serves as the county seat, and it is richly populated in both citizenry and cherished landmarks. It is also a city that was borne of necessity, forged through tenacity and pioneered by privilege.

As the 1830s were dawning, northern Indiana and Marshall County were on the threshold of a most ambitious roadway project. The Michigan Road has since been cited as being one of the primary factors for the population surge that occurred in its wake. And perhaps nowhere is this more evident than in the evolution of Plymouth.

The lands that came to be known as Plymouth were first observed as a potentially charged place for development by the road commissioner of that time, a fellow by the name of William Polk. The responsibility of surveying prospective sites for clearance to allow for the passage of the Michigan Road was one of Polk's great duties in the early 1830s. Upon noticing that the Yellow River intersected at an opportune place along the future Michigan Road, he was inspired to further the cause of creating a city. Polk also boldly suggested, in correspondence with Indian agent John Tipton, that perhaps it would be wise to investigate the possibility of earmarking this new settlement as a future county seat. Polk and Tipton were well versed in matters involving the Michigan Road formation, as it was largely due to Tipton's efforts that the engineering phases of the road were approved by the state and federal jurisdictions.

One of Polk's letters to Tipton from the spring of 1834 expressed tremendous excitement over the fact that many settlers were relocating to the proposed city, and he suggested that erecting a post office there would be worthwhile. The city of Plymouth was first platted in 1834, in right angles to the new Michigan Road, with three individuals bidding $1,000 for the acquisition of sixty-three lots. Within those lots, several were slated for use for the construction of a courthouse square, a schoolhouse, a market house, a seminary and a "burying ground." William Polk was among the men of that trio and was joined by James Blair and John Sering in that groundbreaking purchase, so to speak. Polk is said to be the gentleman who suggested that the community be called Plymouth.

The appointment of Plymouth as the county seat had not yet taken place by this time, as meetings were still being conducted for the purpose of the organization of Marshall County. Such action was finally carried out on February 4, 1836, with the newly seated county commissioners officially selecting Plymouth as the county seat on July 20, 1836.

Shortly before the institution of both Marshall County and Plymouth in name and record, the first store was opened in Plymouth by Oliver Rose—it operated out of a small log structure along what was later called LaPorte Street. His business partner was Gilson S. Cleaveland, who initially worked for Rose as a clerk before taking over sole proprietorship and carrying on Rose's enterprise for a number of years.

That summer, others arrived in town to venture into the business spectrum, including Uriah Metcalf and Milburn Coe. Coe soon cobbled together what was regarded as Marshall County's first sawmill, although it was generally looked on as something of a crudely run facility. The dam that was built to help provide power to the site was designed poorly, and at times of heavy rainfall, there were almost always washouts and flooding concerns. But a primitive mill was perceived as an improvement over not having a mill at all, and so Coe's business continued to turn out doors and window casings. Eventually, enough lumber was produced to allow for the construction of a few frame buildings, but in the end, the problems caused by the haphazardly built dam outweighed the purpose of conscientious work, so the mill was abandoned.

Grove Pomeroy, one of those who benefited from Coe's lumber mill, proceeding to build Plymouth's earliest hotel. It was raised at the corner of Michigan and LaPorte Streets, which were the only two considerable roadways crossing Plymouth's downtown square at that time. Before one of those thoroughfares became known as LaPorte Street, though, it was generally known to the locals as the "Yellow River" road, in relation to its proximity to the river. Both roads were fairly modest, bearing mainly wagon traffic and consisting of dirt paths that became muddy and nearly impassable during inundating rains.

Pomeroy's hotel was initially called the Yellow River Hotel, but the name was later changed to the Plymouth Hotel. The inn was a popular respite for travelers from across the Midwest and beyond, particularly as the formation of the Michigan Road was taking shape. Pomeroy's lodging place was also thought of as a perfect halfway point between Logansport, Indiana, and Niles, Michigan, a north–south trail that was a heavily traveled stage route.

Pomeroy's reputation as a fair and decent landlord who always strived to regally accommodate his guests also accounted for much of his success. The hotel served as a meeting place for executing land sales, and Pomeroy could usually be counted on to extend many courtesies to travelers by way of entertainment. The Plymouth Hotel achieved new levels of notoriety when the section of the Michigan Road corridor was completed through downtown Plymouth. Townsfolk marveled at the arrival of a particular stagecoach driver by the name of "Old" Jake Rhinehart, who would make regular stops in Plymouth amid much fanfare—sounding a tin horn, cracking a whip and leading a spirited team of four horses steering a grand "rock-a-way" coach! Spectators from across the community would go forth to meet the visitors, giving them a cordial reception.

Local historian Daniel McDonald offered a rather jocular view of life in downtown Plymouth in its early days while chronicling Marshall County history in a 1908 publication:

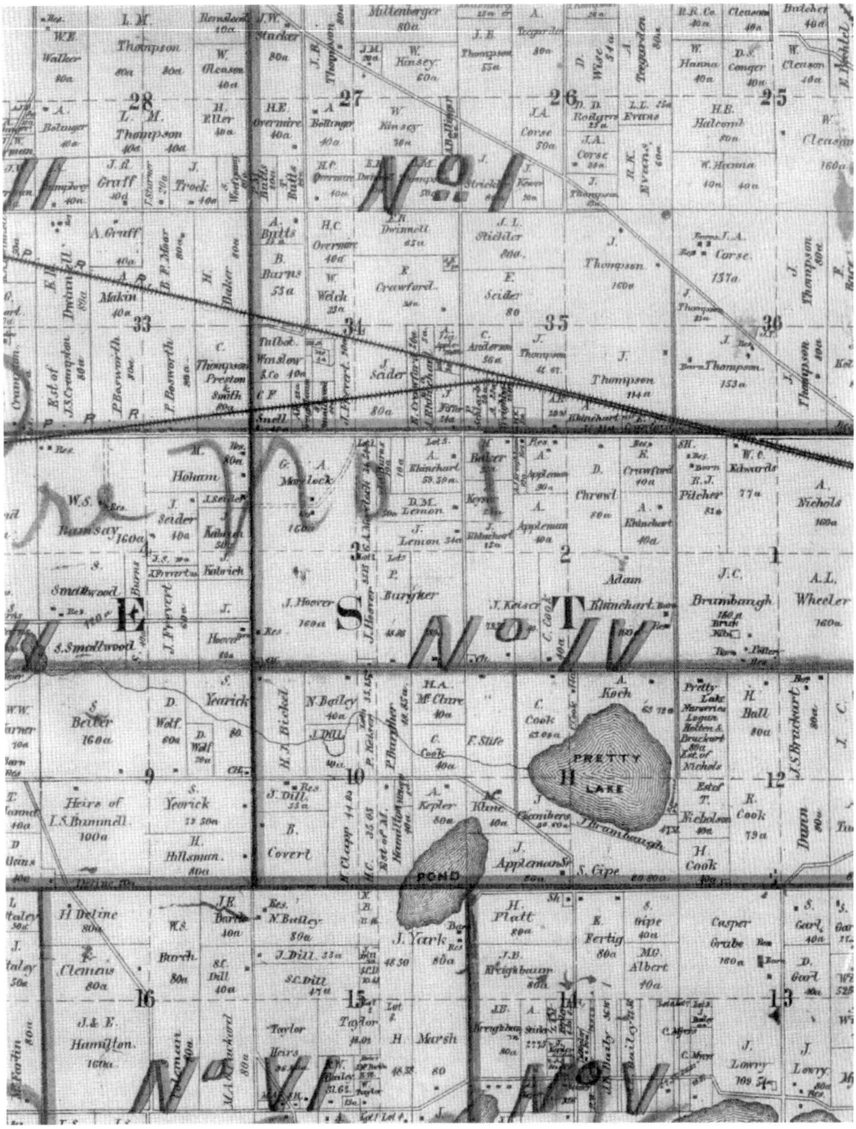

This is a reproduction of a West Township plat map from about the late 1800s. The author's great-great-grandfather, Elijah Crawford, was one of West Township's most established residents. He was the owner of two large sections of farmland, which are located in the northern tier of this map. *Marshall County Historical Museum.*

> *Cows and horses, hogs and other animals had the freedom of the town without let or hindrance. Many of the cows were furnished with bells… they would congregate at some convenient place in the residence part of the village and tinkle, tinkle, tinkle their bells the whole night through, to the disgust of nervous people whose sleep was easily disturbed.* [A]*s has been the case ever since the beginning of the world, is now, and ever shall be, there were numerous dogs…good dogs and bad dogs, yelping dogs, and howling dogs, and just…dogs.*

One particular establishment that garnered quite a reputation as a local "watering hole" was also in operation during this time. Although the creator's name has remained concealed for posterity, it's uncertain what brought about the element of secrecy. Just a short distance from the fledgling Michigan Road, along the south side of the river, visitors could cross a teetering log bridge to gain entrance to a small shanty, which was opened under the guise of a grocery but was well known to locals as the "saloon."

The owner's wares included whiskey, which he obtained from Kentucky and sometimes mixed with other spirits to please the palates of the patrons. As such, the bar was humorously referred to as the "Old Kentuck." It was not uncommon for politicians to gather there and discuss items of importance, always maintaining poise in their carriage and demeanor by not partaking of excessive libations. Much of the conversation drifted toward the Democratic agenda and how to bring esteem back to the party, not unlike a possible topic of debate today.

Other stories indicate that ministers would sometimes visit the Old Kentuck, bringing decanters and filling them on the premise of providing "spiritual food" for their parishioners. Farmers sometimes kept their "little brown jugs" as readily accessible to them as water, and physicians often kept a batch of the liquor on hand to treat sicknesses and other common maladies of the residents, which sometimes included snakebites.

Plymouth's first jailhouse was erected in 1838 and was located at the southwest corner of the area now known as Courthouse Square. The first jail was a two-story structure fashioned from hand-hewn logs—with no door on the first floor. The second story featured a trapdoor in the floor through which prisoners could be lowered into the ground level. Having no entrance and exit points on the ground floor helped to ensure that the criminals could not escape. This building was to be replaced by a new jail in 1851, but the new structure was so crudely designed that the potential for flight risks among lawbreaking vagrants was high. So a sturdier brick jail was planned and was available for use by 1879, built at a cost of $16,970. It was located at the juncture of Center and Madison Streets, where it remained in service until a new Marshall County building was opened in 1974.

The town's first courthouse was situated on Michigan Road, between Jefferson and Adams, and began servicing the citizens of Plymouth in 1840. It would later be replaced by a second courthouse. The present Marshall County Courthouse, the third one built, was unveiled in 1872. It has remained one of Plymouth's most recognized landmarks, grandiose in its form and beauty.

An artist's rendering of the Marshall County Courthouse, not long after the completion of its construction in 1872. *Marshall County Historical Museum.*

One nearby lot, situated on Plum Street, was set aside for future use as a county seminary, with an additional tract located on the west side of Plum Street earmarked for a public burial site. When the first resident of Plymouth passed away, the body was mistakenly placed in the lot designated for the seminary, owing to the fact that there had been some confusion between the similarities of the terms "cemetery" and "seminary." The mix-up was discovered later when plans came to light to build a school on the seminary lot. So the graves of those previously buried were exhumed and moved to where they were originally supposed to end up, only to be reburied yet again when the railroad cut through the cemetery. This time, the bodies were taken to the south end of town, where they were at last laid to rest at the Oak Hill Cemetery.

The formality of Plymouth being a town corporation was approved by a charter granted by the state legislature on February 11, 1851. Records from that time period, which would have provided greater details about the acts and the results thereof, were lost in a fire that consumed much of the Michigan Street business corridor a few years later. It is known, however, that Rufus Brown was the first president of the town board.

Early businesses from that time period could generally be found along one of Plymouth's main thoroughfares—Michigan, LaPorte or Center Streets—which when intertwined made up the greater share of the downtown sector. Proprietors included H. Pierce, who was one of the first men of the community to sell men's clothing, along with lathes and shingles. He and other clothing merchants would sometimes travel to Pittsburgh and New York to procure the latest trends in men's fashion.

Lauer's Men's Store was another prominent men's apparel store and operated under the ownership of brothers Meyer and Levi Lauer. The pair came to Plymouth in 1858 but had no plans to take up permanent residency in Plymouth initially. Their first venture was a general merchandise store, which opened in 1861 on the west side of Michigan Street, between Garro and LaPorte Streets. When the brothers dissolved their partnership in 1881, Meyer Lauer soldiered on with the sales of men's fine clothing until his death in 1904. His son, Moses, who had been assisting his father since 1891, took over the helm and remained until his death in 1944.

The Lauer name lives on among Plymouth's current downtown sector, as Moses Lauer and his brother, Leopold, created a building bearing their family name in 1911, choosing a site at the southwest corner of Michigan and Garro Streets. The larger facility allowed new generations of the Lauer men to carry on with the tradition of offering high-end men's fashion, and they were joined by Moses's son, Marc, who partnered with the elders in 1919. Marc's son-in-law, Henry Paskin, continued the affiliation with the business until it finally closed its doors in 1982. The Lauer building now features a tradition of a different sort—providing the residents of Marshall County with countless vintage treasures of the greatest resources, photographs and memorabilia of the region. It has been the home of the Marshall County Historical Museum since 1993.

Other tradesmen and salesmen were erecting shops downtown in the second half of the nineteenth century, with many of the store owners juggling more than one vocation. Postmaster J.F. VanValkenburg bought hides at the local post office, undertaker A. Boyd sold chain pumps, Judge Fuller ran a flour mill and a lumber dealer named William Shively bought quantities of butter, eggs and timber. Some of the storefronts sported unusual façades, with sculpted and artistically rendered symbols for ease of recognition as to what their specialties were: a horse's head would signify a harness shop, a boot would indicate the shop of a shoemaker or boot maker and wooden Indians were the preferred advertising medium for tobacco shops. Two tobacco merchants, Bob Rudonski and Hans Herter, would often become frustrated at the arrival of Halloween, when their wooden Indians would disappear from the store exterior in a wave of holiday mischief.

Another one of Plymouth's most enduring fashion entities was Bosworth's, founded by Frank Bosworth in 1891. He began the business as the F.W. Bosworth Company along LaPorte Street, later moving his store to 203 North Michigan Street, enlarging the facility over time by adding to the original building. Bosworth's was one of the county's leading merchants in the distribution of women's and children's apparel, bedding, linens, fabric, notions and other related accessories. The store continued for nearly a century, with Bosworth's grandson, William Laramore, assisting with the operation under new ownership when the final sale was held in 1982.

Fate would deliver a cruel blow to a city still very much in its infancy through two devastating fires, which came about just over five years apart and created catastrophic damage. The first blaze was discovered smoldering in the early morning hours of December 16, 1851, originating in a building on the east side of Michigan Street, surrounded by a frigid winter backdrop in which the temperatures had dipped well below zero. The flames quickly spread to other businesses on the block, and residents turned out in droves to salvage what merchandise they could before the sparks gave way to a raging inferno. The ladies of town were said to be among those of valuable assistance, as they often used their long dresses to scoop and carry items outside. One woman, identified only as Mrs. Rhinehart, even stood on a countertop while flames approached with dangerous speed, tossing wares to waiting hands below.

Much of the block was considered a total loss, but thanks to the valiant efforts of many, the losses to inventory were greatly reduced. The *Plymouth Pilot* ran a lengthy article describing the scene of the fire in the next day's edition and offered high praise to the women of Plymouth for their bravery.

A little more than five years later, in the wee hours of March 22, 1857, the same block experienced another disastrous fire. The alarm sounded at 1:00 a.m., rousing citizens, who expeditiously arrived on scene to provide aid. In a scenario reminiscent of the fire that had taken place just a few years earlier, the masses sprung into action by tossing furniture and goods to the streets. This time, though, the weather was waging war against their courageous work, with high winds from the northeast providing fuel to the flames. As a result, not only were the stores leveled, but much of the merchandise that was so hard-fought to recover was also burned. Among the items lost were all of the records pertaining to the founding and the early years of Plymouth. The entire block between LaPorte and Garro Streets was reduced to cinders.

The fires were the impetus for the creation of Plymouth's first fire department, with a two-story firehouse rising up at the riverbank on the south side of Adams Street. The first floor was where the fire equipment was kept, while the second story was set aside for meeting space. A four-wheeled wagon, a handful of twenty-foot ladders and a large iron hook with a loop attached were the first pieces of firefighting apparatus. The latter was used to pick apart a burning structure and scatter about the debris to try to extinguish the fire more quickly. Three cisterns were also created—two along Center Street and another on Michigan Street near Washington Street—in which water was kept. However, evaporation was a problem, and it became too costly to continue refilling the wells, so the cisterns were scrapped.

A second fire station was presented to the community in February 1876, with a festive atmosphere surrounding its debut. A grandiose reception and ball were held, and the public was welcomed to celebrate the new building with sophistication and style. As before, the lower level was used to store equipment, while the second story was sectioned into two rooms. One room was a meeting place for the firefighters, while the other room had office space for the mayor and city clerk and chambers for the city council. The historic building is still in use today as the Marshall County Convention and Visitors Bureau.

Education and enlightenment were priorities of the highest concern for the residents of Plymouth, and there were efforts to begin a public library as far back as 1837. The Marshall County Library Association was formed on October 7 of that year. With a small selection of books on hand, a borrowing schedule was soon put in place—one-hundred-page books had to be returned within one week, two hundred pages warranted a two-week grace period and so forth. By 1845, the county commissioners took over the operations, followed by reorganization a few years succeeding, when the county clerk, auditor and recorder were named to a board of managers. The recorder was also appointed as the librarian, and the books were kept in his office. But by 1900, there were fewer than fifty books in the rotation, as folks were not vigilant about returning items in a timely fashion. As there were no funds available to replace the lost items, the board of commissioners subsequently disbanded the library.

The public did have another option, though, as the public school library was organized in 1880 under the auspices of the superintendent and the board of education. One librarian was hired, with a salary funded through a local tax levy. This enabled residents and schoolchildren alike to have the services of a public library, however small.

Plymouth's Methodist Episcopal church, as depicted in this picture postcard from the late nineteenth century. *From the historical archives of Amy Wenger.*

By 1910, a group of impassioned citizens began lobbying for interest and money to erect a new public library for the city. The impromptu library board contacted Andrew Carnegie, who pledged an amount of $15,000 to help with building costs. The final project tally, including the building and its amenities, came to about $17,000. The townspeople welcomed the new library with abundant fanfare, even hosting a parade during the laying of the cornerstone on July 7, 1913. The new library was completed and opened to the public on January 29, 1914. It remained Plymouth's public library until 1977, when the current library facility was created.

Plymouth's Centennial Opera House became one of the county's premier venues for entertainment from across the county and the country. Located at the south side of LaPorte Street between Michigan and Center Streets, the hall was typically resonating with presentations ranging from literary to spiritual to dramatic and anything in between. Another popular gathering place for folks was the Methodist church on the southwest corner of LaPorte and Center Streets, a popular outlet for many concerts. Many organizations were founded in the middle to latter part of the 1800s and, while too numerous to list, had a wide spectrum of interests ranging anywhere from social to musical to patriotic, with many residents belonging to at least one club.

Politics always provided a spirited platform for debate and discussion and, more often than not, led to viewpoints that would sometimes polarize the town. Passions for one affiliation or the other were so strong that even in death the beliefs of the deceased were interestingly conveyed to the public. A long-held notion from previous historical accounts illustrates the idea that when local newspapers printed death notices of the departed, the wording would take note of a person's political stance, and if a person did not belong to the party that was currently being endorsed by that particular paper, the obituary simply would not appear.

On the issue of newspapers, as it were, Plymouth has had at least one regular publication for almost 150 years. The longest of these, which will soon mark its 150th anniversary observance, is the *Plymouth Pilot*. The paper was founded by John Q. Howell, who originally hailed from Rochester. In 1851, Howell moved his printing press to Plymouth and

Daniel Morlock and family, as seen circa 1900. Morlock's wife, the former Fannie Crawford, was a sister to the author's great-grandfather. Members of the Morlock family were prominent citizens of Plymouth, and Daniel, an ardent Democrat, was quite active in a number of civic organizations. Daniel and Fannie are shown with their three children, Cora (standing), Claude (at left) and Lester. *Karen Crawford Lant.*

created the original printed news outlet for the community. The first issue was dated April 16, 1851, and numbered "13," in an effort to preserve the continuance of its former readership in the city of Rochester, which subscribed to the former *Rochester Republican.*

From then on, the newspaper was subjected to a dizzying array of ownerships and name shuffling. Howell sold the *Pilot* to Richard Corbelay in March 1852. Corbelay promptly changed the name of the paper to the *Plymouth Banner* and changed its political affiliation from Democrat to Whig. Corbelay was not particularly well versed in matters of overseeing the publication, however, and his stint as editor was very short-lived. He handed over the reins to William J. Burns, to whom the paper was sold in July 1853.

Burns was said to be a true "newspaper man" and was successful in reinvigorating the publication and transforming it back into a formidable news source. For reasons unknown, Burns turned over his share of the *Banner* to Thomas Thompson, the deputy sheriff at that time, whose motives were believed to be purely political. Thompson hired James Wickizer to assist him and later named William G. Pomeroy to the editorship. Because none of these gentlemen knew the schematics of running a news organization, they tossed their veritable hot potato back to William Burns in March 1855.

The office was then sold to John Greer in the summer of 1856, during the height of the Buchanan-Fremont presidential campaign. Greer was a key representative of the local Republican Central committee, but his tenure as editor lasted only a few weeks, before he sold his paper to Ignatius Mattingly that same year. One of Mattingly's first orders of business was to rename the paper the *Marshall County Republican.*

More than a dozen years (and more than as many editors and publishers) later, the paper's name was changed yet again, first to the *Plymouth Republican* and then to the *Plymouth Daily Tribune.* Years later, the original name of the *Pilot* was restored, and thus remains the city's only daily newspaper celebrating more than one hundred years of continuously providing news to the people of Plymouth.

Today, the *Pilot-News* is one of several newspapers under the ownership of the Pilot News Group, which oversees the operation of a number of newspapers across Marshall County. Of these, the *Pilot* is currently the lone daily paper, with the other papers distributed weekly, including the *Bremen Enquirer*; the *Leader* of Starke County; the *Culver Citizen*; the *Bourbon News-Mirror*; the *Advance-News*, serving the Wakarusa and Nappanee region; and the *Shopper*, a free advertising circular that reaches readers in Marshall and Starke Counties.

The *Marshall County Democrat* was a separate publication that was organized by Thomas McDonald and his two sons, Daniel and Platt, in 1855. Daniel McDonald became editor in 1857 and, along with his brother, called the weekly paper *McDonald & Brother*. The paper changed hands a number of times during the course of the Civil War, when the paper itself nearly became something of a casualty to the battle.

Known as the *Plymouth Weekly Democrat* by 1863, the editor D.E. VanValkenburgh committed an egregious judgment call by allowing the printing of a scathing criticism of General Milo Hascall, which VanValkenburgh himself authored. VanValkenburgh took great offense at the appointment of Hascall to the "district of Indiana," a position that gave Hascall free authority to censor all avenues of the media. VanValkenburgh's blistering retort to this development read, in part, "Brig. Gen. Hascall is a donkey—an unmitigated, unqualified donkey, and his bray is loud, long, and harmless; merely offensive to the ear; merely tends to create a temporary irritation."

Considerably outraged, General Hascall sent a fleet of soldiers to VanValkenburgh's residence, rousing him at 4:00 a.m. and proceeding to take him under arrest. After first appearing in Indianapolis to face the consequences, VanValkenburgh was then ordered to appear before General Burnside in Cincinnati. After a few minutes of deliberation, it was determined that VanValkenburgh's offense did not rise to the level of federal prosecution. However, VanValkenburgh was reprimanded harshly and admonished with the order never to call General Hascall a "donkey" again.

Amazingly, that incident did not signal the end of the *Democrat*. More editors came and went, with the purchase of a new steam engine powered cylinder press in 1875 signaling the advancement of news publication. To showcase the new equipment, the first written history of Marshall

County until that point in time was released in February 1876. It featured pictures, maps and historical information and was called the *Centennial Democrat.* By 1902, yet another change came to pass. The Honorable Clay W. Metsker published two newspapers—the weekly *Plymouth Democrat* and the daily *Plymouth Independent.*

Daniel McDonald—who was affiliated with the paper that he helped create in some fashion or another over those many years—later achieved recognition as a respected historian, writer and civic leader. While retaining his interest in the publication of news, a handful of other, smaller papers rose and fell, including the *Mail and Magnet*, the *Indiana Greenbacker*, the *Restitution*, the *Farmer's Monthly*, the *Church Monitor*, the *Sunshine* and the *Plymouth Chronicle.*

There was once a small newspaper that predated the *Plymouth Pilot* and that was noted briefly in a single letter issued to the *Pilot* in the fall of 1851. The author of the note, signed only as "Allen," congratulates the editor on his newfound success and makes a reference to a circulation called the *Plymouth Journal.* "The *Plymouth Journal* survived but for a day," the letter noted, "as it were Whig in politics, it died in time to be buried by the proper political party by 1845." The lone copy, dating back to 1844, exists on microfilm at the Marshall County Historical Museum.

Turning to the subject of education, schools of the town were consistently provided dating back to the time of Plymouth's inception. A number of individual scholars of the area graciously allowed their own homes to be transformed into makeshift schools, while others took use of unoccupied cabins, in an effort to educate the community's youth. One of the first teachers noted by name was Thomas McDonald, who taught lessons in a log home that was previously lived in by a farming family near Lake Maxinkuckee. Most of the region's other schools were brought about in proximity to where the people were living at any given time, with children attending the school that was situated closest to home.

The town's first public school was taught by Oscar F. Norton in 1837, with classes conducted in the local courthouse at the corner of Michigan and Adams Streets. Earlier discussions about constructing a school on the land set aside for a seminary finally came to fruition in 1854, with the construction of the town's first schoolhouse. By 1874, a larger building, known as the Washington School, was built, featuring three classrooms and a recitation hall. The school was enlarged through a series of additions in 1893 that enabled the building to house students in all grade levels.

The former schoolhouse that preceded Washington School was relocated to the east end of the Yellow River on Washington Street and outfitted for use as a flour mill, which was called the "Eureka Mills." The milling complex was lost in a fire several years later.

The Washington School was enlarged through an addition project that took place in 1893. The building was then adequately able to house students in all grade levels. Other schools that were located in the outlying area of rural Plymouth were the South Ward School, built in the early 1870s at the intersection of Webster and Miner Streets. Originally designed to house students in grades one through eight, the building was later sold and moved to a new site at Michigan and Pennsylvania Streets, with the Webster School being built in its stead. A portion of the original schoolhouse, erected in 1897, still stands at that location. The West Township School was built by 1889, replacing an earlier structure built prior to 1872. It was not considered a part of the Plymouth town school system, though, but was rather a nearby elementary school before being converted into a high school by 1907.

With the population rising dramatically by the early 1870s, Plymouth was finally given affirmation to function as an official city and was furthermore entitled to function under the principles of such. The formal institution took place in 1873, and in May, the city elected its first mayor, Horace Corbin. Corbin's former place of residence remains in town and is located at 913 North Michigan Street.

Among the items up for discussion during the first few meetings of the Plymouth City Council was the establishment of the assessed valuation of the community, which was tabulated at $700,000. A $20,000 bond issue was also set for the construction of the Washington School, and a great deal of discussion centered on the need for a viaduct to be constructed on South Michigan Street. That project came to completion one year later.

The very first claim paid out was in the amount of $31.25 and was issued on June 9, 1873, to Mrs. E. Dawes, for reimbursement of rental costs on the firehouse. The council members also drafted an ordinance prohibiting swine from running loose on the streets of downtown Plymouth. Another ordinance established a dog tax, with citizens required to pay $1.00 for each male dog and $2.00 for a female dog. Still another ordinance was written outlining the protection of Plymouth's shade trees.

Within a few years of that first election, Plymouth was illuminated by the installation of electric lights for both private and public use. A waterworks was also created at the community's disposal for a variety of uses, at last giving citizens some peace of mind for sufficient fire protection.

A new age was coming to Plymouth, and to America as a whole, as the 1900s bowed. Advances in transportation, communication and utilities were driving forces behind Plymouth's enormous commercial and industrial growth. Several blocks of the Michigan Street corridor, as well as many auxiliary side streets, were devoted to a veritable wealth of businesses. Even the most all-encompassing roster would still not do them justice, but to touch on a few interests, there were restaurants and diners, places of worship, hardware and machinery outlets, pharmacies, furniture retailers and apparel stores. And grocery stores actually sold edible items, as opposed to being a cover for excessive imbibing, as was the case some fifty years ago.

Plymouth was one of three cities to be selected for a pilot project in the mid-1920s that involved Montgomery Ward and Company. The firm was already a familiar and established entity, having achieved more than fifty years of service as a mail-order business. The firm's humble beginnings dated back to 1874, when Aaron Montgomery Ward printed his first catalogue—an eight- by twelve-inch flyer with thirty items available for purchase.

Ward chose Plymouth—along with Marysville, Kansas, and Little Falls, Minnesota—to become "merchandise exhibit" stores. This allowed folks to see the merchandise before they committed to ordering. Several businessmen of Plymouth were fascinated by this idea and opted to begin purchasing samples, thus launching the first Montgomery Ward retail outlet in the United States. The department store remained a fixture in Plymouth until its closing in 1973 but continued on with a catalogue order auxiliary until the 1980s.

A scene from the shores of Pretty Lake, located just southwest of Plymouth on State Road 17. It is known to be a popular place for ice fishing among local anglers. *From the historical archives of Amy Wenger.*

Recreational opportunities also blossomed during this time, with perhaps the most famous of these being Centennial Park. The land on which the park now winds along was a former fairground on Plymouth's north side. When the state of Indiana observed its 100th anniversary in 1916, the aptly named local park was opened to the public for the first time. A stone archway that graces the Michigan Street entrance was built by Bert Ackles under a project funded through the Work Projects Administration, an employment endeavor launched by President Franklin Delano Roosevelt. The gateway was dedicated on Independence Day 1936. In 1973, fifty-seven acres across the river were added and joined to the original park by a covered bridge. The new expanse of park property allowed for the addition of baseball diamonds, tennis courts, a heated swimming pool, picnic tables, basketball hoops and courts and a shaded play area, all surrounded by the color and beauty of seemingly endless flowering and flowing gardens.

The former site of the Zehner Grist Mill near the Yellow River was purchased in the late 1930s and developed for use as another public park.

The WPA sponsored another construction project, this time adding a new clubhouse, which is still in use. The area, called Magnetic Park, features a lovely centerpiece of a stone canopy sheltering a flowing well. On the west side of town, patrons could visit Packard Woods, perched between Madison and Harrison Streets. At one time, this was where children annually commemorated the conclusion of the school year by indulging in a picnic. Eventually, the city bought the property, and the lot was redeveloped into a National Guard station along the south end, with a new playground located at the north side.

Price Memorial Park, located north of town on the Plymouth-Goshen Trail, is a privately owned reserve featuring a lake covering three acres as well as breathtaking landscaping. Access to the park is granted by special permission only. A number of smaller playgrounds geared toward the use of younger visitors are scattered about town, and their maintenance falls under the jurisdiction of the parks department.

With Plymouth continuing to experience a surge in population well into the early twentieth century, a need for a reorganization of the schools soon became evident. In 1924, the $250,000 campus of the Lincoln High School was completed, with four more rooms added on by 1949. This marked the debut of Plymouth's first public high school. Meanwhile, Washington School, which had formerly housed pupils in all grade levels, was redefined as an elementary school. Franklin Elementary, once located in the former Brightside Orphanages school on Michigan Street north of Plymouth, was also a short-lived part of the local school network.

In the decades that followed, more developments in the community necessitated still more changes. Jefferson Elementary School was the next school launched, located on the eastern fringe of Centennial Park, by 1950. The building was a single-story unit with six classrooms, a multipurpose room, an office and a health suite. Six more rooms and a multipurpose room would be added in 1962.

The construction of Plymouth High School in 1960 coincided with the first talks that raised the possibility for consolidation. By 1962, the merging of West Township and Center Township with the city of Plymouth had commenced, and the school system became Plymouth Community Schools. The campus of Plymouth High School remains at its original location on Randolph Street and was created at a price of just over $1.5 million. The design included four "units" within a court plan. Unit One, a two-story area, was where the main lobby, administrative section, library and several classrooms oriented to basic fields of study could be found. The second unit, on the south and southeastern side, was geared toward the agricultural, industrial and homemaking arts, languages and other fine arts. Unit Three featured a teacher's lounge, a cafeteria and kitchen, a music room, a "cafetorium" and a "student book room." The final unit, at the northeast corner, primarily housed the physical education department. Many changes and additions have taken place in the fifty years since the doors first opened.

The West Township School, which had been designated a high school in 1907, was taken back to its initial idea to serve as an elementary school by 1965, and it was attended by students in kindergarten through grade five. In 1970, a newer, more modern Washington School was constructed where Oak Road and Lake Avenue meet. The old Washington School was razed and transformed into Garden Court, a neighborhood for senior citizens. The final days of the West Township School came to pass by the early 1990s, when it would be replaced by the Menominee Elementary School, now called Riverside Elementary, which found its home on Baker Street in 1993.

More than a century after the first traces of Plymouth were rising up in the county, the mission of its primary developers had wavered little—how best to encourage and recruit employment opportunities for the community. By the 1950s, although Plymouth's provenance was greatly improved since its earliest days, many of its residents were compelled to find jobs in nearby larger cities, such as South Bend and Warsaw.

Thus, the group PIDCO, the Plymouth Industrial Development Corporation, was formed. Its focus was to find and purchase land, erect new buildings and sell them to interested parties looking toward expansion. To accomplish this, it first sold two thousand shares of stock, at fifty dollars per share, to help secure funding to lend businesses hoping to invest in Plymouth. Several companies jumped at the prospect and later became part of one of Plymouth's most vital industrial sectors. The early businesses included Bomarko, MidAmerica Containers, Young

Door (later called Doorcraft of Indiana) and New World Products, renamed Norwesco.

PIDCO continues to remain an active force in luring new business to Plymouth, more than half a century after its debut. It continues alliances with such organizations as the Indiana Economic Development Corporation and other governing boards of Marshall County, offering a variety of incentive opportunities to present and future corporations and companies.

As one might expect with a city of Plymouth's stature, there have been a number of local and nationally recognized celebrities that have proudly called Plymouth their hometown. Actor Ken Lackey, a native of Plymouth, was born in 1901 and was a graduate of Plymouth High School. Lackey is credited as being one of the original "Three Stooges," appearing alongside Moe (Shorowitz) Howard and his brother, Shemp, in 1923. The trio was billed as a vaudeville act at the time, long before the television series of the same name became popular. Lackey later returned to his home state and began a distinguished career in politics, serving under three separate judges of northern Indiana before his passing in 1976.

A beloved comic actor of the 1930s and 1940s was born in Plymouth as well. Raymond Walburn moved to California after high school, followed by his mother, to pursue fame and fortune. After a rocky start in a number of theatrical productions, Walburn finally ascended to national prominence in the late 1920s, working under such esteemed directors as Frank Capra. His acting career was interrupted by his time in the military, yet in the span of a few decades, he managed to perform in over one hundred films. His unique facial features and somewhat bombastic gestures earned him comparisons to the character of "Mr. Monopoly," the wide-eyed, mustachioed snub-nosed fellow who is featured in the board game. Walburn died in 1969 in New York, not long after having resurrected his career on the Broadway stage during the 1960s.

Still another familiar, more contemporary, face in Hollywood had roots in Plymouth—the actor Richard Bergman. In the well-received 1980s family show *Father Murphy*, Bergman left perhaps his most memorable impression, in the role of Father Joe Parker. Bergman also appeared in *The Love Boat*, *Days of Our Lives* and *Highway to Heaven*.

St. Michael's Catholic Church, as it appeared in the early twentieth century. The cornerstone for this church was laid in 1910, although the Catholic body of worship is one of Plymouth's oldest, dating back to 1856, when the membership gathered in homes and other simple structures. The church was instrumental in the creation of St. Michael's Academy, which remains a private educational institution of high regard in Plymouth. St. Michael's presently has one of the largest congregations in the community, with more than one thousand families in regular attendance. *From the historical archives of Amy Wenger.*

Plymouth's longtime reputation for its outstanding athletic prowess peaked with a number of championship titles achieved by several teams during the second half of the twentieth century. The Plymouth High School football gridiron greats took home a state title in 1977, while the boys' basketball team nabbed a win in the 1982 state contest. Led by standout Scott Skiles, the squad won a hard-fought battle in double overtime, 75–74, over Gary Roosevelt High School. The basketball team of the 2006–7 season was also victorious at the state level, taking the win over Evansville Bosse with a 72–61 final. The Plymouth girls' basketball team also brought home a state title in 2008 in the class 3-A division, edging out Indianapolis Bishop Chatard by a score of 47–46.

Most recently, Plymouth returned to the national spotlight in June of 2007 when 2003 PHS graduate Nicole Rash was crowned Miss Indiana, a first for the community. She had also competed for the honor of Miss

Ball State, capturing that crown as well, being the first contestant in Ball State's history to win the Miss Indiana title. Rash advanced to the Miss America competition in January 2008 and was chosen as the first runner-up. Rash now resides in California, where she hopes to continue to cultivate her talents as an aspiring singer and actress.

Three annual festivals take place in Plymouth, all of which present their own interpretation of the community's heritage and history. The newest of these is the Yellow River Festival, which takes place on the first Saturday in June and celebrates the American Indian nuances and influences of the region, along with the area's history prior to 1860. Also fairly recently instituted is the Heart and Hands Latino Festival, held on the third Saturday in June at the Young Amphitheater in Centennial Park. Visitors can sample Latin American cuisine and be surrounded by the sounds of Hispanic music. The children's area is a large draw, as are the artisan booths, the silent auction and the demonstrations from area businesses and vendors. The event is sponsored by Heart and Hands, Inc., which serves as an outreach for the Hispanic community by providing job training, classes and diversity awareness programs.

The largest and longest-running attraction in the trio of festivals is the Blueberry Festival, which dominates the Labor Day weekend and creates an atmosphere of such magnitude as to rank second only to the Indianapolis 500 in terms of its size. Dozens of musical acts, a large parade, the Blueberry Stomp marathon, a large volume of sporting competitions and other features add to the excitement. And, of course, there is an abundance of food, much of which includes blueberries. Since its 1966 inception, the Blueberry Festival now welcomes guests to Plymouth to the tune of 500,000 attendees.

CHAPTER 6

FROM DONALDSON TO LAPAZ, TIPPECANOE TO TYNER

A Tapestry of Towns

The intertwining rural roads of Marshall County not only offer passage through the region's most prominent cities but also provide glimpses into many small boroughs that may appear diminutive in size but are mightily impressive for the impressions and the contributions they have imparted among the chronicles of history. The many stories from yesteryear, which have been shared through countless generations, still reverberate strongly within the hearts of residents both former and present.

BURR OAK

Within one of Marshall County's earliest-organized townships lies a little gem known as Burr Oak. It was in and around this area where some of the very first artifacts were found pertaining to, and possibly predating, Indian culture.

Burr Oak's plat was recorded on December 15, 1882, by Michael Burns, who is listed as proprietor. Conservatively built to include eighteen lots, with a small volume of streets and alleyways, it was laid out along the Nickel Plate Railroad in Union Township. Franklin Overmyer filed a request for an additional plat on October 8, 1885, with eight more lots slated for placement just east of the Burr Oak station.

Considerable notoriety was given to this region, which was also referred to as the "Burr Oak Flats," when several mounds were discovered southwest of the main square. The development of these rounded piles of earth was said to be the work of early Mound Builders, and several excavation efforts were launched at differing points in time, as prospectors worked to determine exactly what the curious-looking mounds were used for. When traces of what appeared to be human bones were revealed, it was theorized that perhaps the American Indians had crafted the mounds for burial purposes, though that idea was mostly debunked, as this was not a typical means in which the Potawatomis left their deceased.

At that time, scholars who claimed to be well versed in the ways of the Mound Builders projected their claims that perhaps the mounds were utilized as primitive shelters, perhaps while gravitating to warmer climates in abandonment of the frigid Indiana winters. Over the years that have followed, further discoveries of items such as tools and pottery suggests the possibility of the mounds being used simply for storage. Because no established records were ever kept concerning the expeditions of the amateur explorers, the mystery of the mounds continues to this day.

DONALDSON

On the western fringe of Marshall County, almost perfectly situated between the northern and southern boundaries, lies West Township, which has a very interesting headline in the annals of local lore. It is the only township that features exactly one small town, that being the burg of Donaldson.

Several resources indicate that one of the first white men to arrive in West Township was Robert Evans, who established himself in the region about 1835. Evans continued his residency throughout the remainder of his life, at one time recalling of the Potawatomis still inhabiting the land that they were "relations…of the friendliest character." Other early families who settled in the township during the same era were the Johnsons, Olsons, Baums, Swansons and Peirsons.

In the following years, several families of German, Swedish and Irish origin, including those previously named, arrived and set about operating family farms. However, they first had to embark on the task of clearing open spaces amid the heavily wooded region, replete with poplar and walnut trees. The timber was promptly shipped to Chicago by way of the newly laid Pennsylvania Railroad, once known as the Pittsburgh, Fort Wayne and Chicago Line.

Much of the wood was siphoned through the business of Charles Swindell, who launched the first steam sawmill in 1859. Because the demand for the lumber was so great, Swindell's primary function was to assist in the preparation of wood for shipment. This he accomplished by reducing the large logs to four-foot lengths, which would then be positioned along the tracks. As the trains stopped to gather the wood, the planks could easily be tossed to the waiting rail workers to transport. The sawmill also produced railroad ties and cordwood for the rail company.

The overabundance of trees posed one problem, and the fact that much of the area was beneath water posed another. Not to be discouraged, many of the farmers simply began growing what was called "marsh hay." This provided a very lucrative opportunity for resident W.W. Warnes, who built a barn exclusively for the crop and sold the harvested hay to a glass factory in Pittsburgh. The company made use of the hay as packing material.

With the completion of the railroad came a dramatic rise in residency and business interests. Eventually, the modest settlement included a post office, a schoolhouse, a depot, a telegraph tower and a creamery. Three general stores were in full operation in succeeding years. One was run by the Harrison family, another by the Burgeners brothers (Samuel and Peter) and still another by Silas Joseph.

Later additions to the thriving community were a barbershop, a pool hall, a doctor's office, a blacksmith shop, two churches and, perhaps most notoriously, a pickling station for the Heinz Pickle Company, one of many that would be scattered about the region. Another early businessman and resident, George Uncapher, had a successful store in the region beginning about 1868. It has been noted that during the first one hundred years of Donaldson's existence, nearly each of the leading citizens about town had, at one time or another, served as the local postmaster.

The date listed for Donaldson's birth as an incorporated town is October 25, 1871. As to whom the official title of originator should go, however, it should rightfully belong to several individuals. D.W. Taft, Cornelius Tuttle and W.J. Richardson are named as the creators of the town's first plat, which featured twenty-two lots measuring 66 feet by 132 feet. They chose to call the new town Donelson, in remembrance of a Civil War battle in which the men had fought.

By 1875, the town was doubled in size by "Taft's addition to the town of Donelson," with the inclusion of twenty-one additional lots that were similarly proportioned and situated northwest of the original town.. Not to be outdone, Tuttle also drafted "Tuttle's addition to Donelson" on the very same day, September 14, 1875, and created twenty-two new lots at the opposite side of the town.

The vast expanse of marshland that had saturated the community for so long was finally drained in the 1880s, which piqued the interest of more Swedish and German immigrants, who saw the potential for farming the revived landscape. Even so, Donelson, which was renamed Donaldson at an undetermined point in time by the local post office, always managed to keep its small-town ambience, something that local historian Daniel McDonald prophetically spoke of in a 1908 publication revealing the early days of the county. "It is a quiet little village and probably will always remain so," McDonald mused at the time.

Donaldson's business environment changed with the popularity of automobile travel—a truck repair service, two filling stations and a garage sprung up in town. The arrival of the Lincoln Highway was also a tremendous boon, with John Stringer seeing the advantage to be had by opening a hotel in Donaldson. Several trains still made stops in the area, including one that carried the mail, and passenger service was still very much in use. When the Lincoln Highway, more commonly called U.S. 30, was included in a bypass effort in 1963, the new road skirted the small downtown sector entirely.

Over time, however, the town was diminished in its commercial aspect, although it most definitely has not faded in existence. Donaldson is now known as the home of Ancilla College, one of northern Indiana's premier commuter colleges.

The college's Catholic foundation can be traced back to the efforts of Catherine Kasper, born in Germany in 1850. Kasper founded the order of the Ancilla Domini nuns, known as the Poor Handmaids of Jesus Christ, or PHJC. About 1868, Bishop John Henry Luers of Fort Wayne spearheaded a missionary movement by eight of the sisters, which led to their arrival in north central Indiana. Their goal was to provide an orphanage ministry.

By 1918, the PHJC purchased the former Lake Gilbraith Hotel from Chicago wine merchant Louis Glunz, with the purpose of developing the area into a main residence, or "motherhouse," for the sisterhood. Ground was broken for construction the following year, ideally and perhaps divinely suited along the tranquil shore of Lake Gilbraith.

At present, Ancilla College currently has an enrollment of more than one thousand commuter students, and the institution takes immense pride in blending its liberal arts curriculum with career preparedness. The campus includes the Catherine Kasper Home for retired Sisters, Earthworks, the Lindenwood retreat center and the Maria Center for independent living.

Donaldson's only other foray into the realms of higher learning began as a college seminary for the Priests of the Sacred Heart. The land on which the campus was located was deeded to the priests by Clara Mey in 1934, and construction soon began for a twenty-five-acre complex of buildings to house and educate members of the ministry. The school existed for more than four decades until it closed and the property was sold in 1979. It is now known as the Divine Heart Seminary.

Inwood

Inwood is among the absolute smallest of Marshall County's enclaves, still listed as an unincorporated town with an undefined number of residents. But its importance is surely not diminished among tales of the towns.

Located about seven miles east of Plymouth, the community was founded by Ezra Pearson, who came to the area in 1854 and platted the land on December 29 of that year. Pearson christened the town with his own family name, allowing the settlement to be known as Pearsonville. Seeing the potential for good farmland, thus bringing about more farmers, Pearson set about the task of helping to clear the land and was reputed as having the area's first sawmill.

Pearsonville seemed destined for such a prime location when the arrival of the Pittsburgh, Fort Wayne and Chicago Railroad, also called the Pennsylvania line, laid new tracks through the town about 1858. However, the associates for the rail company were not particularly fond of the name Pearsonville, deeming the moniker too lengthy. After some consideration, the name of Inwood was chosen, as the new community was still very much considered to be "in the woods."

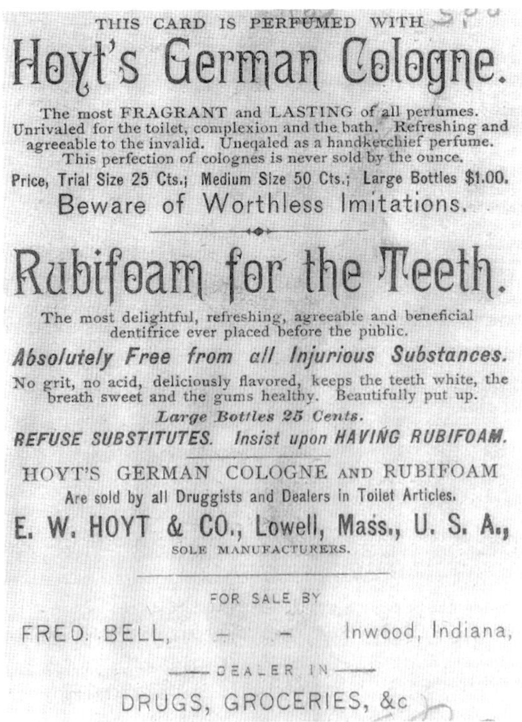

This advertisement by Inwood druggist Fred Bell strikes a rather humorous chord today, given the interesting wording of the message. *Marshall County Historical Museum.*

By the early 1900s, Inwood was a thriving small town, with about three hundred folks in residence, and was becoming rapidly renowned for the quality of lumber production. Several individuals designed additions that were aligned with the original plat, including Pearson's first and second, A.W. Hendricks, Croup & Core's first and second, Frederickson's and Lee & Dickinson's. The little village had a two-story brick schoolhouse, a drugstore, a Methodist church, a telegraph office and various small stores, along with saloons, mills, manufacturers and physician's offices.

As the golden ages of railroading began to pass by, so did the dynamic of the community, which had been so reliant on the transportation of lumber. Property owners shifted their priorities to that of an agricultural nature, and businesses began to disappear. Today, Inwood remains a community primarily in name and through its spirit.

LaPaz

When South American native Archalaus "Achilles" Hunt arrived in northern Indiana in the early 1870s after a career spent mining silver, he knew a grand opportunity when he spotted it. It made perfect sense to erect a town right where the Michigan Road and the Baltimore and Ohio Railroad crossed paths. And so Hunt did just that, creating the town of LaPaz, located about six miles due north of Plymouth and encompassing 121 lots. It was laid out and platted by Hunt on August 5, 1873, and the name he chose was a nod to his Bolivian heritage, the English interpretation meaning "the peace."

While describing the placement of LaPaz in his records, he cited an enormous maple tree reigning on the west side of the Michigan Road as something of a starting point for his dimensions, a tree that was later called the "witness tree." His claim followed the Baltimore and Ohio Railroad, which lay parallel to the Michigan Road, to a point just south of a mail stop called Walnut Hill, about half a mile away. The railroad, also part of the Pennsylvania line, was a pivotal point in service to and

Left: This picture postcard depicts the former B&O Railroad depot in LaPaz, circa 1915. *Marshall County Historical Museum.*

Below: Fred H. Myers, the former county treasurer, was the owner and proprietor of this well-visited LaPaz landmark—the Myers General Store—during the early twentieth century. *Marshall County Historical Museum.*

from Chicago. The Baltimore and Ohio rail company would name a coach in the town's honor in 1949.

By September 1875, Edson Spencer had arrived and platted several more tracts, a total of eighteen lots measuring 40 feet by 120 feet. Spencer called this "Spencer's Addition to LaPaz," which also included streets of about 40 feet in width and a handful of alleys 14 feet wide.

Sadly, a freak accident claimed the life of the man who was credited for being the first settler of LaPaz, and he was never able to witness any future growth. Hunt was killed in 1876 while attempting to lead his horse to water. Hunt's animal kicked him with such ferocity that it resulted in his death.

Moses Thayer was the next individual to arrive in town and organize another redrawing of boundaries. On December 27, 1881, Thayer tacked on another thirty-five lots, to be known as "Moses Thayer's Addition to LaPaz." Less than three years later, during the summer of 1884, Thayer pieced together eleven more lots just west of his original addition. A few months later, in the spring of 1885, Leonard and Gideon Logan laid out "Logan's Addition to LaPaz," which included sixty-four more lots and was situated on the southeast section of town. LaPaz would grow significantly in the years leading up to the turn of the century, not only due to an increase in residency, but also because the area became something of a resort town during the summer months.

At the time, agriculture was the predominant means of earning a living, with mint farming prevalent around the nearby Lake of the

The employees of the LaPaz Grain Company, in a photograph dated 1932. *From left*: Foster Albert, Howard Hill, Orville "Ram" Clark, unknown, unknown, unknown, Glen Wilson, Chester Hill, Chris (last name not listed) and unknown. *Marshall County Historical Museum.*

An assemblage of men takes on the daunting task of breaking up massive chunks of ice that had coagulated in the frigid waters of Lake of the Woods in this undated photograph possibly from the early twentieth century. *Mr. and Mrs. R.T. Henke.*

Woods. One of Marshall County's largest lakes, Lake of the Woods lies within both German Township, near Bremen, and in North Township, closer to LaPaz. The Indians once called the lake "Copenuckconbes," which translates to the name of a beetlike vegetable that was found in abundance there. The Indians of the area, at the time of their habitation there, were known to partake of the unusual vegetable quite often, which was said to rise spontaneously from the marshy, muddy waters along the shoreline. To prepare the food for proper consumption, the Indians would burrow trenches into the damp ground, place stones along the walls and leave an open space near the center in which they placed the copenuckconbes. They would then cover the trenches with leaves and other burning elements and then set the makeshift oven afire, cooking the vegetables in the process.

LaPaz had something of a predecessor with the tiny town of East LaPaz, which was founded by Walter Kimble in 1855. Kimble chose a site about three-quarters of a mile east of present-day LaPaz because of its proximity to the nearby railroads, at a point where the Baltimore and Ohio and the

Along the west side of U.S. 31, newly constructed in LaPaz during the time of this photograph, was this service station owned by Bill Emmons. His daughter, Julia Emmons Herford, is shown in front. *Marshall County Historical Museum.*

Logansport and Terre Haute Railroads intersected. East LaPaz was one Marshall County stop along the Vandalia transportation line.

The dissolution of East LaPaz by the early twentieth century allowed LaPaz to continue on an upward progression for growth and success. Aside from its relevance to the changing times, LaPaz has taken pride in maintaining the small-town atmosphere that charmed residents a century ago, even with the inclusion of the Michigan Road (U.S. 31) as its primary thoroughfare through the center of town.

LaPaz and its northernmost neighbor in St. Joseph County, the city of Lakeville, are connected by a consolidation of schools. The movement to merge the township schools occurred on July 1, 1962, with the organization later known as the United-North-United School Corporation. Currently, the children of LaPaz are transported to the LaVille Elementary School in Lakeville, with the LaVille Junior-Senior High School located nearby.

Above: The former LaPaz High School, before the consolidation of the LaPaz and Lakeville School Systems transpired in 1962. *Marshall County Historical Museum.*

Left: The residence of Dale W. Miller, notary public and justice of the peace for the LaPaz community, as seen in this 1973 image. *Marshall County Historical Museum.*

The creation of the high school was a front-page news item shortly before its unveiling, although not for a reason of positive commemoration. During Indiana's legendary Palm Sunday outbreak of April 11, 1965, LaPaz took a direct hit from one of many tornadoes that cut massive paths of destruction throughout northern Indiana. The LaVille Junior-Senior High School, just weeks shy of completion, was severely damaged in a matter of moments by an EF4 monstrosity, undoing months of meticulous construction. Remarkably, enough progress was made to rebuild the school that students were able to begin classes there in the fall of 1965.

Today, the atmosphere of LaPaz and its five hundred or so residents maintain an admirable place both in local history and in its ongoing mission to have progressive visions for the future.

Teegarden

Calvin J. Wright and Eli Taylor are the men responsible for the platting of Teegarden, which was formalized on October 30, 1873. The village began in anticipation of the arrival of the Baltimore and Ohio Railroad, which would be passing through Polk Township. The name was said to be taken from the name of a local doctor who owned land in LaPorte County but who was a prominent resident of nearby LaPaz.

When the railroad was completed in 1874, Lewis Lemert added fifteen lots to the original layout of thirty-three. Soon, the young town featured two general stores, a sawmill, a kiln and a blacksmith shop. Four passenger trains stopped at Teegarden's depot on a daily basis, and by the turn of the century, more businesses were added to the downtown area, including a jewelry store, a watchmaker, an implement store, a grocery, a livery barn and two tile mills. It was noted by one former resident of the area, a fellow named Millard Lemert, that in the year 1914 everyone in Teegarden owned their own home. Charles Lemert, Millard's grandfather, was the proprietor of the town's first Ford agency in 1908.

When train service was discontinued in the town of Teegarden, it seemingly also swept away what was once a busy, bustling hamlet. Several churches remained in the community, as did the Polk Township Volunteer Fire Department. The old Teegarden School was vacated during the consolidation of the Tyner, Teegarden and Walkerton Schools in 1964 and functioned for a short while as a nursing home facility. Until the consolidation, high school students of the town attended Polk Township High School in Tyner. The merging of the school systems resulted in the formation of the Polk-Lincoln-Johnson School Corporation.

One of the last major businesses to close in Teegarden was the grain elevator, which was destroyed in an enormous fire that occurred on July 26, 1975. That event was said to be pivotal in that it was something of a symbolic movement toward the local economy being brought to a standstill.

Yet despite its diminished profile among the larger towns of Marshall County, the friendships, families and neighborhoods of Teegarden remain, as well as the memories that bind many generations in its unity.

TIPPECANOE

The hamlet of Tippecanoe is another of Marshall County's most illustrious little towns—small in stature but extremely fascinating in relation to its regional history.

Unlike many surrounding communities that sprung up in the mid-1850s, Tippecanoe Township was already fairly well populated by the time pioneers arrived to explore the site. Along the nearby Tippecanoe River and its banks was an American Indian settlement, where some remained who had been exempted from the mass removal of Potawatomis several years prior. A trio of men—Joseph Hall, Daniel C. Martin and Joseph Serls—was responsible for platting and surveying the land, with its resulting incorporation listed as December 12, 1850. The men called the new city Tippecanoe Town. Another early settler, Daniel Bearss, came to the area with his father about 1852 and was said to have had forged good relationships with the neighboring Indians, sometimes joining them on hunting and fishing expeditions.

Shortly after the creation of Tippecanoe Town, the men who were instrumental in its founding were inspired to harness the power of the Tippecanoe River for its prospective use in assisting the milling industry that they hoped to establish. So the men set about constructing a dam, which was a project met with a mixed response from the new residents. Nonetheless, it was an integral force in the rising of several key mills of that time, including a lumber mill as well as a flour mill owned and operated by N.B. and P.S. Alleman. The Allemans also created a woolen mill, which was later sold to J.F. VanValkenburg of Plymouth by 1878.

But the farmers and homesteaders of the village were not happy. Many shared the notion that the stagnant, pooled water caused by the river's dam was creating an increase in the insect population, deeming the pond an "intolerable nuisance." The residents claimed that an increase in sicknesses could be directly attributed to the problem of mosquitoes, which were widely known to carry malaria.

So the disgruntled townsfolk chose to take matters into their own hands, after a number of clandestine meetings had taken place to discuss how best to handle the situation. On the evening of October 25, 1878, under a shroud of darkness, an incognito group of individuals approached the gristmill and attempted to set fire to the factory. However, their attempts were thwarted by a night watchman who was on the premises. In short order, one young man was captured and his innocence compromised when he was accused of being one of the accomplices.

After a spell in the county jail, the lad agreed to profess his guilt and reveal additional names and evidence. By the time the young man was called on to present his story to the grand jury, the prospective perpetrators proved nowhere to be found.

Later that same evening, a second mission to destroy one of Tippecanoe Town's mills was launched, this time proving powerfully successful. The culprits targeted the woolen mill, using an incendiary device to fire upon the building. The flames ravaged the facility with incredible swiftness, leaving only smoldering piles of rubble before assistance could be summoned.

Interestingly, after the event, the first culprit surprisingly materialized from his disappearance. This time, he was able to describe precisely how the act was carried out and also named many of the town's most notable residents as having been among those who participated in the act. The trial that followed lasted for several days and left a great deal of animosity among the residents, particularly directed toward the person who implicated his friends. The jury could not render a decision, and so a second trial was ordered to take place in a neighboring county. However, before that trial could get underway, all of the accused parties fled the county, leaving no indication of their whereabouts, so the case was never brought to a legal conclusion.

Tippecanoe Town had an opportunity to make a fresh start of things when the Nickel Plate Railroad selected the region for inclusion of new tracks by 1881. A new plat was filed on January 9, 1882, by W.W. Burkett, John Kramer, John T. Hardesty, Elizabeth Lewallen and E.J. Martindale and that was located about three-quarters of a mile south of where the first town was situated. A depot was soon built at this site, and within a few years' time, many of the original businesses had opted to move to the new town to be closer to the railway, and the former Tippecanoe Town business district evaporated into obscurity—as had the dam that had caused such ill will and contention.

The newer version of the city was first called Tippecanoe Town Station, but during a December 1886 session of the board of commissioners, a new name was suggested on a petition filed by G.W. Roberts. Permission was granted for the town to be known as Ilion. Only nine years later, the name changed once again, reverting to a shortened form of its previous christening, simply called Tippecanoe. Loyal locals have been known to affectionately refer to the old town site north of the river as Old Tip Town.

Presently, the Tippecanoe area is best regarded for the Potawatomi Wildlife Park, which comprises more than three hundred acres of land near both the Tippecanoe River and State Road 331. It is a privately run institution owned by Potawatomi Park, Inc., and funded through the proceeds of the estate of Vernon Romine.

The wildlife sanctuary features many historically significant sites of the township, such as remnants of American Indian encampments, a section

The Tippecanoe Giants baseball squad, posing for a picture during the 1908 season. *Marshall County Historical Museum.*

of the former Goshen-Logansport Trail and the Tippecanoe River ford, where several Indian paths crossed through the area.

Also located on grounds of the park is an enshrinement to the ways and the life of one of the more infamous leaders of the land, an Indian by the name of Stephen Be-nack (or Benack). Exempted from the mass removal of the Potawatomis from northern Indiana in 1838 because he was not of full Potawatomi origin, several sources list Benack as the overseer of the village that bore his name, an Indian term called "Wkama," or headman. Benack was the original owner of the land on which the park now sits.

Benack's family history has significance not only in Marshall County but in places beyond as well. Benack's daughter, Mary Ann, would go on to marry a fellow by the name of John Peashway, who was also of Indian descent. According to legend, Peashway was a former Miami County resident who arrived in Marshall County to hide after allegedly killing some Indians back in Miami County. Their crime? Stealing Peashway's deer meat.

Because of Peashway's Indian heritage, the white settlers of the area chose to remain outside of the fray, so no criminal charges were ever pursued. Peashway did pay a high price for his crime, however; it was said that his daughter was put to death in an act of retribution.

It has been a little more than a century since the creation of this monument to honor Chief Menominee, one of the most renowned Indian residents of Marshall County. This statue is situated near the Twin Lakes area, where a chapel bearing his name was once located. This photograph was taken during the dedication ceremony in 1909. *Marshall County Historical Museum.*

The Peashway family—which also included a son, Henry—lived on land near the intersection of State Road 10 and State Road 331, which had formerly been owned by Ephraim Bearss. Not far from their homestead was a chapel, which was believed to predate the existence of the permanent chapel that was later erected at the Menominee area near Twin Lakes. According to records at the University of Notre Dame, it was thought that the first church was put in place in an attempt to "impress" the Catholic priests. A monument in honor of Chief Menominee is located at the Twin Lakes site, which was unveiled in 1909. As for the Peashway family, they eventually moved to the Notre Dame area, possibly between 1850 and 1860, and there is supposedly some evidence that many of the family members and descendants are buried in and around the Notre Dame region.

Tyner

When Tyner was in its most vital existence during the second half of the nineteenth century, many of the residents had a level of sophistication that reached national stature. Although Tyner itself is fairly well removed from the scope of Marshall County's larger cities and towns, the generations that have followed those early villagers have continued to harbor respect for those who came before them and contributed greatly to the life and times of Tyner.

The property that eventually became Tyner once belonged to Samuel Miller, who deeded his land to Thomas Tyner on Independence Day 1855. Located about seven miles northwest of Plymouth, the area was platted by Tyner, along with Maynard French and Thomas Miller, later that year. It was to be called Tyner City, in honor of its primary founder.

The Tyner family had a very prestigious pedigree that extended well beyond the boundaries of Tyner City. Tyner himself had a contract to help build the community's first railroad—the Indianapolis, Peru and Fort Wayne Line—which came through town in 1856. Tyner's brother, James, was the postmaster general under the administration of Ulysses S. Grant, a county commissioner during the Civil War and the president of the aforementioned railroad as it extended from LaPorte to Plymouth.

Several of the new roads that were laid out featured the names of many men who were instrumental in helping to build the rail line. Names such as May, Miller, Boyce and French were instituted, with Vine, Main, Walnut and Race being chosen as a nod to Cincinnati, Ohio.

Before long, Tyner City was considered to be a major hub of business and transportation within Polk Township. As was the case with many of its neighboring communities of that same time period, Tyner City proliferated in the lumbering industry and had many thriving sawmills. The Tyner City Post Office was established on September 11, 1856, with Consider Cushman serving as the first postmaster. Squire Cushman is credited for building the first house in Tyner City. A general store soon sprung up near the post office, with the post office being a somewhat unlikely outlet through which folks could purchase candy and tobacco products.

Education was of great importance to the Tyner City leaders and residents. One individual, Professor James G. McGraw, was regarded as a brilliant teacher who became the town's first schoolmaster between 1865 and 1870. So great were his abilities to teach students that word of his reputation reached the ears of a United States senator in Illinois by the name of Nickelson, who attempted to lure McGraw to a post in Illinois. McGraw could not be convinced to leave his community, though, as he had higher ambitions. There were plans between himself and Tyner to create a university near the site of one of the county's many Heinz pickle factories. Another university rose up nearby, which became Valparaiso University, thus hindering any further efforts to build a college near Tyner City. McGraw passed away soon after.

By 1873, Tyner City would become incorporated as a town, but it was a decision rendered with much vitriol and dissension between the townsfolk and the people living in the rural region. As a result of the bickering, no one person was elected to serve in a township office position. A justice of the peace was then agreed on, but within only a few years, the uprising of those against incorporation prevailed, by a twenty-two to eleven vote in an election held on November 29, 1879. The community retained its unincorporated status from that point on.

The following year, Thomas Tyner passed away, on October 18, 1880. Prior to his death, he led the charge to have the archives of the state government relocated from Corydon to Indianapolis when the latter was named as Indiana's state capital. Tyner's loss profoundly affected the small town, with a tribute story later noting, "He was a worthy and highly respected citizen who filled many positions of trust and honor, and always in a satisfactory manner to all parties concerned."

On July 10, 1894, Tyner City became known simply as Tyner. Many years later, Tyner sponsored a grand event that captured and captivated the attention of folks from across America. An open-air theatre was constructed in the park near the town hall, with a "silver screen" erected on a sprawling grassy venue. It was estimated that somewhere between seven and nine hundred people traveled from many states to view this extravaganza, which the local newspaper heralded as a "miracle picture." The first feature that the enraptured crowds watched was called

The Healer, and the reception was so overwhelmingly positive that the local chamber of commerce continued to offer free motion pictures every Monday night for a considerable amount of time to follow. Media reports from that era noted, "Judging from the license plates on some of the cars which visited the performance, the fame of these events had become nationwide, because there were cars from many states of the union."

As the twentieth century progressed, Tyner soon boasted a great range of businesses, including a wooden pump factory, copper shops, a coffin factory, brick kilns, a blacksmith and a stave factory. There was also a cider mill, the previously referenced Heinz pickle factory, a telephone company, hotels and a hardware and lumber company. Tyner had also achieved recognition for being known as the "Huckleberry Emporium of Marshall County."

Between the years of 1920 and 1930, Tyner was also the home of the Farmers State Bank, first organized on June 19, 1920. Stockholders were composed of mainly Polk Township citizens, with the first slate of officers including Albert Burke, president; Carl Wolfe, vice-president; and Charles Miller, cashier. The remaining members of the board were Charles Powell, Earl Bennett, John Johnson, E.O. Samuelson and Dr. A.A. Thompson. Farmers State Bank became a victim of the Great Depression by 1930 and was closed for voluntary liquidation. Some news sources declared that not a single depositor lost funds during the downturn, although a number of persons would dispute this claim.

Tyner's first schoolhouse was a small structure located on Main Street, but it was later replaced with a new building at the corner of Walnut and French Streets in 1902. Subsequent remodeling efforts took place to enlarge the campus during the years 1912, 1928, 1939 and 1955. Until 1966, the facility housed students in all grade levels, but it was later converted for use in grades four and five until 1973.

The commercial landscape had changed by the middle part of the twentieth century, when the community was home to a restaurant, two grocery stores, a garage, an elevator, a barbershop, a printing office, two churches and one local physician. The former post office building was occupied by the Tyner International Order of Odd Fellows until the early 1970s, when the organization built a new lodge. By the 1990s, the former

The former Tyner High School, which first opened in 1902 and underwent several renovations during the decades to follow. It originally housed all students until 1966 and was later a facility for local students in grades four and five until 1973. *Marshall County Historical Museum.*

downtown area featured a grocery and video store, a lamp shop, a beauty parlor and the station for the Polk Township Fire Department; with the exception of the fire department, those businesses have vanished in recent years. Tyner United Methodist stands alone as the last remaining church, Zelma's Beauty Shop lingers in the community and the post office can still be found there.

A CONVERGENCE OF HISTORIC HIGHWAYS AND BYWAYS

Throughout earlier passages of this book, it has been revealed how great of an impression the American Indians and the early European settlers have left in the evolution of Marshall County and its communities. When considering that the region is encompassed by a fairly modest proportion of 450 square miles, it is quite remarkable to discover that there are several legendary highways that pass through the area.

Although the thoroughfares are of national significance today, they certainly were not inspired as such. At the time of and prior to Marshall County's inception, roadways were generally what could be fashioned by the most meager of methods. No engineering, no schematics and no heavy equipment to facilitate the movement of vast quantities of earth. They were once all simple furrowing paths that were crudely devised to navigate from one destination to the next. What follows are the stories spawned from the beginnings of some of Marshall County's most infamous and influential roads.

The Michigan Road

Within a mere ten years of Indiana being included among the states of a young America, there were inklings of negotiation taking place that would lead to the formation of the state's first commissioned north–south highway. James B. Ray was Indiana's governor in 1826 and was also a key proponent for a treaty, signed on October 16, 1826, that dictated the terms of securing a portion of land from the Potawatomi Indians, still among the land's primary residents at that time. The exact specifications are not precisely known, but it was noted that the original concessions would include a strip one hundred feet in width for the road itself, along with one section of land for each mile of roadway for the length of the road in its entirety. The throughway was to extend from Lake Michigan to the west, dip southward toward Indianapolis and then swing northeast to the Ohio River.

The proverbial path to origination, in a manner of speaking, most definitely did not run smoothly. After a lengthy and somewhat contentious period of debating and haranguing by the Indiana state legislature, the selection of 267 parcels for the Michigan Road Lands was finally agreed upon by 1828. The matter of the road itself, however, was a variable in that measurements taken over differing times of survey had a number of inconsistencies. Other matters that proved troublesome included the exact interpretation of the word "contiguous"—whether it should be taken in the context of the treaty as being "lying immediately along," or if it should be taken for the dictionary definition of "being in actual contact." They were seemingly trivial details and yet extremely critical in determining the placement of the road in relation to the existing township boundaries.

Furthermore, there were some discrepancies over how exactly to finance the project. Road Commissioner William Polk was appointed as the principal executor of any further surveys to be conducted beyond 1830. Through correspondence with Indiana's governor and related commissions, it was stipulated that certain sections of land not already bound by the treaty would be sold off to help pay for the Michigan Road. Legislation was drafted in January 1828 advising that the governor share the events with the federal government for further assistance.

In the meantime, it would become Polk's job to earmark suitable sections of land to be procured by interested parties for reasonable rates. But Polk was questioning exactly how to proceed; he was unsure of whether he should follow the survey put forth by his own state or to take heed of the "General Government." Polk's answers came forth rather haltingly; several alleged letters to various department heads and state officials were met with supposed indifference and delayed responses.

A complicated tangle of legalese and misinformation began to impede the project further, and the county commissioners received a pointed reply from Governor Ray in which he informed the men that the survey was not completed nor endorsed by federal standards. The commission finally enlisted the help of Indian agent John Tipton, upon the advice of Secretary of War John Barbour, and at last Congress accepted the terms of the 1828 treaty, and the resulting survey carried out by Polk, by 1831.

Polk divided up the proposed roadway lands into five districts between Logansport and Lake Michigan and designated certain tracts to be "let," or sold. He kept diligent records of the work that needed to be accomplished in order to clear the route and left something of a "to do" list for prospective landowners. Among the land issues that would need to be addressed were draining of the existing prairies, clearing of logs and being mindful of the swampy state of the many marshes and bogs.

An early section of the Michigan Road, as seen near the address of 218 South Michigan Street in downtown LaPaz. *Marshall County Historical Museum.*

The available plots in Marshall County were sold off under maneuverings through South Bend. Many of those early contractors included men whose names strike familiarity among local historians: John Walker, Cyrus Taber, Alexander Chamberlin and David Dinwiddie, among others. Sidney Williams, one of Argos's most integral pioneers, was awarded the contract clearing the future Michigan Road from Rochester to South Bend in 1832.

As construction commenced, Polk observed a natural juncture at which the road was aligned with the Yellow River and that was later inspired to acquire land that would eventually come to be known as the city of Plymouth. Several early schoolhouses, inns, taverns and businesses soon rose up along the fledgling roadway, and by 1832, the first traces of the Michigan Road were at last channeled through Marshall County. Much of the land surrounding the road was still being sold off in market for a few years following, with typical bids running between four and five dollars per acre.

In 1834, the first section of the Michigan Road, which connected Logansport to the end path at Michigan City, was unveiled. The state declared in 1838 that there would be no more funding appropriated for any further aspects of the project, but by that time land sales had quite nearly reached the total amount needed to sufficiently finance the construction. Expenses were calculated at just over $242,000, and the total receipts were about $241,300.

However, there were problems that became evident within only a few years' time. The road, still relatively new, was already beginning to show signs of wear. Oak timbers provided its foundation, along with a foot or so of damp soil procured from nearby ditches, which covered the trail. This was a process known as "corduroying." But traveling by wagon was proving cumbersome on the path, as uneven sections caused horses to jolt and slip along, and farmers quickly realized that this simply would not be beneficial to them in transporting their goods.

Stuck in a literal quagmire, much intervention would have to come about for the road to ever reach "highway" status. The Indiana General Assembly passed a measure in 1836 called the Indiana Mammoth Internal Improvement Act, which would allow $10 million in state funds for the improvement of the state's infrastructure with regards to transportation. But the next year brought a catastrophic event called the Panic of 1837, when the nation's banks ceased payments on gold and silver, rendering many states at that time nearly bankrupt, Indiana being among them. As a result, further direction and guidance on how best to proceed with the completion of the Michigan was left to the counties and private enterprises. By 1846, the Indiana state legislature granted permission for the Logansport and Rochester Michigan Road Company to resume construction of the road line between Rochester and Plymouth. During that time, many of the earlier sections of road that were deemed impassable were reworked with the inclusion of planks to bolster both appearance and function.

When the Michigan Road was finally completed by the mid-1850s, it was considered the main conduit for travel between northern Indiana and its capital city of Indianapolis. Much of the thoroughfare had come under private ownership, and it became each entity's responsibility to oversee road conditions. Gravel constituted the preferred method of paving by that time, and many sections could only be driven on by

The Michigan Road, as it passed through downtown Argos, in this photograph from the late 1800s. *Marshall County Historical Museum.*

passengers willing to pay a toll. Having a steady stream of incoming funds would help to ensure that maintenance would always be of utmost priority and concern.

The advent of automobiles shifted the focus back to state ownership, as the usage of vehicles rapidly overshadowed wagons as the primary method of travel. Much of Indiana's Michigan Road corridor would make the transition to pavement by the 1930s, and as speed limits were introduced and enforced, many sections of the roadway were realigned to deviate somewhat from the original layout, in accordance with the prevalence of cities, towns and other principal areas of commerce.

Much of the Michigan Road, which has been called "Indiana's first superhighway," follows the course of the current U.S. 31 corridor, which is one of the nation's longest north–south multiple-lane roads, extending from northern Michigan to the southern end of Alabama. A number of offshoots from the original road are now state- or federally designated routes and interstates, such as State Road 29, Interstate 65, U.S. 421 and Interstate 465 encircling Indianapolis. Throughout the state, though, there are many stretches of roadway that have remained relatively unblemished and true to the spirit in which they were created, most notably in the southern part of Indiana. Farther downstate, there are fourteen counties that are still considered to be part of the Michigan Road lands, where early covered bridges, two-lane ribbons of unmarked pavement and other landmarks spanning almost two hundred years of state history can still be found.

The Grand Army of the Republic Highway

The Grand Army of the Republic Highway is mostly recognized by its designation as an east–west road in the U.S. highway system, more commonly referred to as U.S. 6. In its present state, U.S. 6 is regarded as the second-longest highway in America, beginning its slightly northeast ascent in Bishop, California, and ending in Provincetown, Massachusetts. With relation to Marshall County, U.S. 6 currently runs mostly parallel to the northernmost edge of the county, skirting the northern rural fringe of Bremen and passing just south of LaPaz, where it intersects with U.S. 31.

Before it became the Grand Army of the Republic Highway, or even U.S. 6, however, the road was a slight and short path connecting Brewster, New York, to the Cape Cod region in Massachusetts. As the 1920s and 1930s saw an increase in the construction of state- and federally sponsored highways, the future U.S. 6 was extended westward during various phases in time and in many sections in a gradual fashion. This patchwork of mostly rural passages led to the conclusion by one particular commentator of the era to remark that the lengthening of the roadway left travelers venturing from "nowhere to nowhere."

By October 1925, the Joint Board on Interstate Highways issued a recommendation to include the proposed multilane road within a seventy-six-thousand-mile web of trails that would be a numbered national route. Roads running east to west would be given an even number, while north–south thoroughfares would receive an odd number. U.S. 6 was the proffered name from that time forward, with a few minor modifications to the route occurring in the late 1920s and early 1930s. The section that passed through Marshall County was completed and paved in 1932. U.S. 6 officially became a transcontinental highway, completing its final stretch to the California community of Long Beach in June 1937.

Other names that U.S. 6 was known by in those days included the Midland Trail Roadway and the Roosevelt Highway, so named for President Theodore Roosevelt.

It would take almost twenty years before the first suggestion to honor U.S. 6 with its Grand Army of the Republic christening would become a realization. In 1934, U.S. Army major William L. Anderson Jr. conceived of the idea of the name, in tribute to the Union forces of the Civil War. Spirited by this recommendation, the Sons of Union Veterans of the Civil War began actively campaigning for the passage of the title by April of that same year. But because the highway was still owned by each of the consecutive states through which it passed, every state would have to sign the endorsement to the effort, a process that took more than ten years. The Hoosier State offered its official vote of approval in 1946.

Travelers along U.S. Highway 6, also known as the Grand Army of the Republic Highway, were sometimes compelled to stop and dine at this unique Bremen eatery, known as the Coffee Pot. The restaurant was the creation of Elmer Laudeman, who fashioned this dining facility from an old wooden silo in 1932, having seen a similar building pictured in an edition of *Popular Mechanics.* The interior of the eighteen-foot-diameter structure featured an appropriately styled round counter. The attraction was considered an ideal midway point between Ohio and Illinois and was so successful that an addition was pieced together in the late 1940s. Eventually, the silo fell into disrepair and was later purchased and demolished by the State of Indiana to clear the way for the U.S. Highway 6 Bypass north of Bremen. *Mr. and Mrs. R.T. Henke.*

A formal dedication of the Grand Army of the Republic Highway was held on May 3, 1953, in Long Beach, California. Representatives from the Sons of Union Veterans of the Civil War were on hand to witness the presentation of the designation that they had so passionately lobbied for. A monument was then placed at the Municipal Auditorium that read, in part, "In memory of the heroic services and unselfish devotion of the Union soldiers, sailors, and marines who laid down their lives on the altar of sacrifice during the Civil War...For what they did and dared, let us remember them today."

The highway as it pertains to Marshall County originally passed through downtown Bremen, where it remained situated for several decades. But by the early 1970s, a stream of thought was beginning to flow, with the belief that the very same roadway that kept local, regional and national travelers flowing through town was also the very same roadway that was creating traffic headaches as larger-scale vehicles and semis attempted to move along the narrow downtown streets. During the year 1973 alone, there were 7 fatalities, 54 injurious accidents and 183 incidents of property damage, all said to have taken place on account of the heavy volume of traffic.

A public forum was held on May 4, 1973, during which the topic of a possible U.S. 6 Bypass was broached for the first time. Residents, retailers and representatives from the business sector were on hand to hear input from several federal and state organizations. All were hoping to voice concerns and hear suggestions in the hopes that their fears would be allayed—how could transportation needs be met without sacrificing the heart of Bremen's downtown? It was discovered that the majority of people in attendance were in favor of a bypass, although no one wanted to see the new route stray too far from the original U.S. 6 design. The project was subsequently added to the Indiana Department of Highways work program during the 1971–73 biennium.

Three proposed bypass routes were presented at that initial open meeting, including one that would take U.S. 6 on a southern jog around the town. The route that was eventually approved would take the bypass on a northern path, with an exit juncture near the Yellow River just beyond the Miami Road intersection, west of town. The new road would ascend slightly northeastward, with an overpass along State Road 331, until ending at another exit immediately past the Bremen Cemetery on the east end of town. Another point of exit would be designed to channel traffic either northbound or southbound at the Elm Road exchange.

After more than a decade of construction and planning, the new U.S. 6 Bypass was dedicated and permitted for use on June 30, 1982. This author has many fond memories of the evolution of this project, which unfolded not far from the neighborhood in which she was raised. On more than one occasion, she could be counted among many eager youngsters who delighted in bicycling along the wide, pristine new highway, oftentimes stopping at the stately overpass to stop and wave at the rather bewildered motorists driving along below on State Road 331.

Several years later, the former section of U.S. 6, which ran through downtown Bremen, was renamed State Road 106, and the route continues to run concurrently with the roadway with its more common name, Plymouth Street.

The Yellowstone Trail

When considering that the Yellowstone Trail, in its primary role, was only well utilized for a span of twelve years, it seems even more remarkable that it made an appearance among the open spaces of Marshall County.

The Yellowstone Trail is defined as being the first transcontinental highway in the northern third tier of the United States that was designed exclusively for automobile use. It was conceived by a fellow named J.W. Parmley, a businessman of substantial esteem from Ipswich, South Dakota. Parmley and his colleagues desired a suitable route to transport them from their home city to Aberdeen, South Dakota, a distance of about twenty-six miles.

Soon, the idea of extending the road westward to Yellowstone National Park was brought forth, hence the inspiration for the name of the trail. Shortly thereafter, a group was formed called the Yellowstone Trail Association and was headquartered in Minneapolis. The organization did not oversee the actual specifics of the road construction but instead elected to have delegates and cities designated for inclusion along the route. Representatives would, in turn, assist in carrying out the pledge to have local workers create and maintain the new highway. They would also serve as lobbyists to the local branches of governments, taking up the cause to convince their leaders to appropriate tax dollars toward the cause.

Those workers typically consisted of businessmen, blue-collar workers and members from participating chambers of commerce, but the locals were also enthused to lend their assistance. Cities and towns sometimes sponsored occasional "Trail Days," with a joyful atmosphere, celebrations of food and music and the closing of businesses to allow as many individuals to participate as were able. The jovial backdrop was said to be something of a distraction from the hard work of "dragging" the dirt road.

Communities along the route would also be required to pay dues to the association in exchange for the production of promotional materials, such as maps and flyers, which would allow an influx of tourists to the sites along the trail. Volunteers took on the task of appropriately marking the route with obvious dashes of color, such as bright yellow stones or through the use of the association's logo, a yellow circle emblazoned with a black arrow.

Eventually, the association's mission would be producing "a good road from Plymouth Rock to Puget Sound," truly, a coast-to-coast adventure.

By 1916, the *Plymouth Republican* announced that the first hints of interest were being voiced to have the Yellowstone Trail cross Marshall County. In May of that year, delegates from the Columbia City Commercial Club arrived in Plymouth to share their allegiance to the project and, in keeping with the festive sentiment, were accompanied by the Columbia City Band to regale the crowd with music. They also brought along an "ice cream car," from which two thousand ice cream cones were passed out to an enraptured audience.

"This section of Indiana is the best in the state," the *Republican* article declared, "and should this road go through it, it will put us on the map in good shape."

It would take another four years, however, before the State Highway Commission would endorse the designation for the Yellowstone Trail as it meandered through the county. The commission sanctioned a section of path along the Leesburg Road north through Plymouth, west through Donaldson and Hamlet and along the current 12B Road south of Inwood before joining another westward road that would take travelers on to Valparaiso.

Keeping up appearances along the local stretch of the Yellowstone Trail was more than challenging, though; many folks later reminisced in journals and news accounts about the extremely poor condition of the road. Barely distinguishable among a border of yellow stones and stakes, the trail consisted of a gummy, pasty soil that often caked up around buggy tires. Many a weary and frustrated wagon driver was forced to stop and chip away at the residue, which was labeled "gumbo" by many exasperated residents and travelers.

Sadly, the Yellowstone Trail as it was originally intended fell victim, in part, to the Great Depression, due to the fact that the bleak economic conditions rendered many communities and merchants unable to pay their association dues, thus leaving no financing to continue on with the necessary upkeep. Also, the American Association of State Highway Officials had only recently begun with its national effort to have a numbered highway system. Only the most well-maintained roads were chosen for inclusion, but the Yellowstone Trail was not among those selected.

The Yellowstone Trail Association is still very much in existence today, now functioning primarily as an organization of historical awareness and preservation. Several of the earliest-created sections are still visible, predominantly in the eastern end of the route, where strips of red brick or gravel still bear the Yellowstone Trail name.

The Lincoln Highway

The Lincoln Highway could be considered the "first of firsts," being that it was the frontrunner in transcontinental travel within the United States. The first highway spanning from one end of America to the other was formally dedicated on October 31, 1913. On the East Coast, its origination was at Times Square in New York, while on the West Coast, its starting point was located at Lincoln Park in San Francisco.

It was the culmination of a dream realized by a powerhouse of American industrialists and led by Carl G. Fisher; it was about one year in the making. Their desire was to present a continuous multiple-lane highway, "open to lawful traffic of all description," which would also be a fitting tribute to former president Abraham Lincoln.

The road was also said to be brought about through the affiliation of the good roads movement, which was an advocacy group led predominantly by bicyclists. The group actively lobbied for improved roads, having long grown frustrated over the condition of much of the nation's paths, trails and highways.

Interestingly, the Lincoln Highway came nowhere near Marshall County at the time of its inception. Beginning near Chicago to the west and crossing the Ohio border by way of Fort Wayne and points southeastward, the midway stretch of the highway had a fairly steep slope northward into the neighboring cities of South Bend and Mishawaka, brushing just south of the Michigan state line before dipping southeast through Elkhart County and the cities of Elkhart, Dunlap and Goshen.

During the gestation period of Lincoln Highway, the road in its entirety was to include 3,389 miles. But by the 1920s, several realignments and removals were made in an effort to streamline the highway and make the path more straightforward. Major changes were implemented within the Hoosier State when a section of the road between Valparaiso and Fort Wayne was redefined. During the process, Marshall County was swept directly to the forefront of the inclusion, with the new Lincoln Highway passing through the heart of the region and into Plymouth, the largest city in the region.

Affectionately called "the Main Street Across America," the Lincoln Highway was among the many major thoroughfares slated for renaming during the national highway numbering system that took place in the mid-1920s. The corridor was designated as U.S. 30, and it is still primarily known as such today. Much of the Lincoln Highway as it originally wound around the northernmost portions of Indiana still bears traces of its place in history, with many of the streets bearing names such as Lincolnway or Lincoln Avenue.

Remembering the Lost Villages of Marshall County

Many a muse and a scholar, as well as every sort of common man in between, has observed that the one variable that remains constant is that there will always be change, in all of its remarkable ways and whims. That certainly bears comparison to the Marshall County that once was and illustrates the journey leading to what it has become. So many villages and boroughs have vanished from the landscape over time, their existence transcended to a somewhat sacred stratosphere of "a place that used to be."

So, with that sentiment in mind, the conclusion of this book shall be devoted to the towns that were, in one way or another, very much a part of Marshall County but will remain forever immortalized in its history.

Blissville

Among the stories of Marshall County's towns that have drifted toward the echoes of days long since passed, the tale of Blissville is perhaps one of the most comical. Initially set along the western edge of Polk Township, the burg was a modest notion originated by Justice T.F. Stevens, a man of considerable clout and very intimidating presence in the region. Stevens erected a store of large proportions, in which he sold dry goods and groceries. Stevens also surmised that perhaps the travel-weary pioneers might enjoy the delights of a saloon, where the whiskey was said to be plentiful and problematic. Stories of drunkenness and debauchery became so commonplace that it prompted one individual to facetiously refer to the settlement as Blissville, and the name stuck. However, there are records to indicate that the town was once called, ironically, Justice.

By 1856, the completion of the Indianapolis, Peru and Chicago (also called the LaPorte) Railroad had occurred, which thereby shifted the center of trade and other commercial prospects to the communities of Tyner and Walkerton. Stevens chose not to relocate his business, and being of an advanced age, he passed away a short while later.

Clayton

The suggestion for this settlement came about shortly after the division of North Township into three separate townships in 1838. The township located farthest to the east was inhabited primarily by residents of German extraction, so the township was named German Township. Seeing the potential for a town in this newly designated region, the first residents—Lanthrop M. Taylor and Henry Augustine—helped to launch the movement in 1837 and decided on the name of Clayton. Two streets were laid out in the formation of an "X" along the paths already existing near the remnants of the Plymouth-Goshen Trail and a second road connecting South Bend to Warsaw.

It was soon realized that this location was not desirable, because it was deemed too far from the center of the township, and so plans for the creation of a settlement were shifted three miles to the west. That marked the beginnings of the town now known as Bremen.

Elizabethtown

Elizabethtown was strictly an institution on paper, its founding and its ending occurring rather simultaneously. The site was platted about halfway between the towns of Plymouth and LaPorte, along the Plymouth-LaPorte Road. Given its situation between the two rapidly growing regions, it seemed like the perfect spot at which to attract new businesses and curious settlers. Meticulously laid out in the shape of a cross on May 23, 1837, by G.A. Cone, it never quite found its pertinence to Marshall County's formation and now exists simply as a matter of record.

Fairmount

Fairmount's story is quite interesting in that it was never exactly a town, though it was the wish of a lone enterprising individual that it would become one.

Although the precise date is not known, there was a time prior to 1900 when a tavern was opened on the Michigan Road about five miles north of Plymouth. The owner was named Silas Higbee, and he christened his new development Fairmount. Field surveyors' notes from 1833 feature the placement of Higbee's tavern.

Higbee's saloon was frequented often until it was destroyed in a fire, and because it was so closely settled to Plymouth, it was not considered advantageous to try and recruit any new opportunities at that location. However, a farmhouse now sits on what is known as Higbee's Corner, and a nearby cemetery and church still bear the name of Fairmount, the town that never was.

Harris Station

Harris is a tiny unincorporated area of North Township, just west of LaPaz. There was one small depot in the site, which was never formally instituted as a town. It was formally platted, although the precise date is not known, and the depot was sometimes manned. The little train station was basically a spot for debarking or boarding the trains.

One of the only landmarks to mark the existence of Harris—this small, plain train depot. *Marshall County Historical Museum.*

Hibbard

Hibbard was the name of a miniscule parcel of land on the western edge of Union Township. The area had a series of strange christenings before becoming known as Hibbard, the designation that was recognized by the local post office. There is apparently no record of exactly when or if the town was ever officially platted, but for reasons never quite articulated, passersby referred to this place as Helltown. Eventually, the name was changed to Dante, supposedly in reference to the Italian poet who wrote "The Inferno," a story of an imaginary journey through hell. Sometime about 1890, the name was changed to Hibbard, and it was the name that stayed.

Now regarded as more of a village in spirit, Hibbard did exhibit signs of interest from settlers by the early 1900s. The heart of the community is now situated where 15B Road and Redwood Road intersect, a few miles northeast of Culver. At one time, Hibbard had its own school, post office, depot and a handful of industries, but the region was fairly abandoned with the coming of the Nickel Plate Railroad, when businesses set their sights on larger cities and towns.

Huckleberry Marsh

In the middle part of the nineteenth century, there was a section of land about three miles west of Tyner that was widely regarded for its lush huckleberry marsh. During the huckleberry harvest, the region was a significant draw for the pioneers, who considered the site something of an encampment for the duration of the season. Several hundred people would set up temporary residence, keeping busy with the business of distributing the berries and securing sizeable profits for all parties involved. Wagons came and went along the one path that connected the march to nearby Tyner, where similar transactions were carried out.

While never officially organized as either a town or a village, the shanty settlement had a most vibrant existence. Any disturbances were thought of as minor, and the relations among the settlers were extremely jovial. There was dancing, gambling, partaking of spirits and music but only very rare incidence of overindulgence, save for a few wayward fires.

By the late 1800s, however, the marshes were being drained, the lands were often burned and the berry crop was disappearing. Seeing no particular reason to continue with the annual tradition of the harvest, the settlement drifted into obscurity.

Linkville

Also listed on older county maps as Linksville, this tiny settlement was the situated on a main road that was located a short distance away from Bremen. It was located about five miles northeast of Plymouth, in the southeastern corner of North Township. Twelve lots were part of the first formal plat, filed by Simon Stough, M.J. Link and E.J. Mosholder on June 9, 1866. It was a most convenient placement to many of the surrounding communities that were developing lumber and sawmills, and for a time, that was also Linkville's largest industry as well. Linkville also boasted a stately brick schoolhouse for eight grade levels. But as other towns experienced increased interest from new residents and businesses, Linkville's relevance was relegated to its scenery.

North Salem

The advent of the railroad caused the extinction of North Salem, which was also known as Lycurgus. Barrack Plummer, Basil Roberts and A.G. Pumphrey banded together to create a plat of twelve lots for the town in 1851 on a site south of Inwood. The region's lone building was a massive, elegantly designed church facility, which was swiftly eradicated in a fire only a few years later. More opportunities were being found in nearby Inwood, which was located in the direct path of the new rail line called the Pittsburgh, Fort Wayne and Chicago track, so businesses were attracted to that town instead. The former heart of the region is now located on 12B Road, where Ironwood intersects. A cemetery is situated near Hawthorne Road, and a lone store was once found at the corner of Juniper and 12B Roads.

Panama

Isaac Shively is the lone individual responsible for the organization of Panama, which was platted on September 6, 1854. The hub of the timber industry, it was located about five miles northeast of Bourbon on the former Plymouth-Warsaw Road. Growth did not come about as expected, although it did not prevent Jacob Pritch and Adam Moneysmith from settling in Panama a few years after its origin. The men built a sawmill there, which served as the ideal conduit for the passage of timber, allowing the men to excel in the exchange of lumber. Panama also had a modest boardinghouse for the sawmill workers' temporary residence.

For a time, it seemed as though Panama might finally be revealed as a prospective community, even capturing the attention of local politicians who sometimes used Panama as the setting for various campaign functions. But once all of the trees were cut down and removed from the landscape, it appeared that the settlers went with it, and the village dissolved before the arrival of the twentieth century.

Rutland

Rutland was almost close enough to its Union Township neighbor, Hibbard, to be considered a sister city. Rutland was a small grouping of buildings and settlers located one mile southeast of Hibbard and was intended to grow with the advent of the Nickel Plate Railroad. However, Rutland's population never quite materialized beyond what could be accommodated by a post office, a schoolhouse, a church, a lone store and a railroad station.

Sligo

When this small section of West Township was first organized, it was believed that a few white settlers came to the area from the state of New York and decided to name a town after Onondaga, their former county of residence back east. Although the names of those men were never recorded, the first successful business of the town, a gristmill, was launched by Timothy Barber about 1836.

Within a short time, the region had a schoolhouse, a post office, several stores and shops and one church. Bog iron was found in great quantity around this site, so the Old Forge was built to proliferate and maximize this resource. The business was run by two men from South Bend—Charles Crocker and French Fisher. Crocker decided to abandon his ownership in 1850 when he was lured by the promise of gold mining farther west.

Crocker's departure ushered in a period of decline for the town, which had been renamed Sligo, the inspiration for the name being unknown and unrecorded. The gristmill ceased operations, and the Old Forge company experienced a decrease in productivity. Since the latter was not able to turn out a respectable amount of business, it was no longer deemed profitable to continue hauling the wares to and from South Bend, and the industry fell by the wayside. The remnants of the gristmill were removed in 1922 just as the last of the Sligo woods was being cleared away.

Walnut

This tiny burg was located twelve miles south of Plymouth and was laid out in a series of eighty-three lots on April 16, 1866, along the path of what was to be the Lake Erie and Western Railroad. It was first called Fredericksburg, named for its chief proprietor, Frederick Stair. Two years later, when the railroad was completed, representatives expressed a preference for calling the town Walnut, and it became so. Two individuals by the last names of Calhoun and Tucker made some alterations to the town by adding more lots several years after its creation.

Residents of the area sometimes referred to the town as "Possum Trot," due to the sheer volume of opossums that frequented the region. Frederick Stair, a well-respected man who was said to be a friend to all who knew him, died in the 1890s, and as it would appear, so did any aspirations for the town to rise to prominence other than in name only.

Wolf Creek

Not quite a town but more significant than a settlement, Wolf Creek was a place that met with a rather tragic demise. Wolf Creek was the name of a tiny place on a winding creek about five miles south of Plymouth. Prior to 1840, a dam was built in the creek, and a water-powered sawmill was erected. A white pioneer by the name of Clark Bliven became the sole operator and founder of a small gristmill. He called the area Bermingham, as was recorded in a petition filed with the board of commissioners. Bliven was hoping to implement a road that would connect the Michigan Road through his new town and then extend farther west to the reservation of Missinoquah (Miss-in-oquah) on the Yellow River. Missinoquah was a female Potawatomi spiritual leader (recorded as a "chieftainess") who was already quite elderly when Bliven arrived in the region, but he respected the tribe enough to ensure that a treaty would be drafted allowing for the retention of their land. Missinoquah was among those who were carried away in the exodus of the Potawatomi tribe in 1838, and her later whereabouts were never known. The very creek that Bliven believed would provide a livelihood for the village was the very one that ultimately claimed his life—he drowned during an episode of high water only a few years later, and thus he and any hopes for the town's future were swept away.

BIBLIOGRAPHY

All of the information used—including books, archived newspapers and more—can be found at the Marshall County Historical Museum in Plymouth, Indiana.

Books/Booklets

Argos Sesquicentennial 1851–2001. Commemorative book published in 2001, with excerpts used from Wayne VanDerWeele's 1951 book.

Bourbon, Indiana—Bicentennial Celebration, 1976. Published by the Bourbon Bicentennial Festival Committee, 1976.

Bourbon, Indiana, 1853–2003: A Historical Past, Fascinating Present and a Bright Future...Celebrate the Journey. Published by the Bourbon Sesquicentennial Committee, 2003.

McDonald, Daniel. *History of Lake Maxinkuckee.* Published in cooperation with the Maxinkuckee Lake Association. Indianapolis, IN: Levey Bros. & Co., Inc., 1905.

———. *History of Marshall County, 1836 to 1880.* Chicago, IL: Kingman Bros., 1881.

———. *A Twentieth Century History of Marshall County, Indiana.* Chicago, IL: Lewis Publishing Co., 1908.

Rettig, Marwood, Reverend. *Centennial '71...The First One Hundred Years of Bremen, Indiana.* Published by the Bremen Centennial Committee, 1971.

VanDerWeele, Wayne J. *Argos Centennial 1851–1951.* Published by the Argos Centennial Committee as a commemorative booklet, 1951.

NEWSPAPERS

Bremen Enquirer
Plymouth (IN) Daily Tribune
Plymouth (IN) Pilot

OTHER SOURCES

Gaines, Aaron. "History of Marshall County." Plymouth, IN: Marshall County Historical Society, 1998. Essay written, compiled and distributed through the historical society. Gaines was formerly the assistant director of the Marshall County Historical Museum in 1998.

Hunter, Juanita. "Marshall County & the Michigan Road." *Marshall County Historical Society Quarterly Newsletter* 20, no. 2 (1991).

Weingroff, Richard F. "U.S. 6: The Grand Army of the Republic Highway." Published and distributed through the archives of the U.S. Department of Transportation's Federal Highway Administration.

ABOUT THE AUTHOR

Amy Wenger has been working professionally as a freelance writer since the age of sixteen, beginning her newspaper career at the *Bremen Enquirer* while still in high school. Nearly twenty-five years later, her writings have appeared in a number of area newspapers spanning across four northern Indiana counties. She continues to contribute feature stories and articles of historical significance to several publications. In 2004, Amy received recognition from the Nappanee Historic Preservation Commission when she was honored with one of the city's first awards for historic preservation education. She has two other books on regional history still in circulation: one focusing on Elkhart, Indiana, and the other on southwestern Elkhart County. Amy currently resides in Wakarusa, Indiana, with her husband, Larry, and their three children, Hannah, Rebekah and Josiah. In her spare time, she enjoys genealogy, reading and spending time with family and friends.